BARRON'S BUSINESS LIBRARY

Publicity and Public Relations

BARRON'S BUSINESS LIBRARY

Publicity and Public Relations

Dorothy I. Doty

BARRON'S

All inquiries should be addressed to:
Barron's Educational Series, Inc.
250 Wireless Boulevard
Hauppauge, NY 11788

International Standard Book No. 0-8120-4413-4

Library of Congress Catalog Card No. 90-37819

Library of Congress Cataloging-in-Publication Data

Doty. Dorothy I.
   Publicity and public relations / by Dorothy I. Doty.
   (Barron's business library)
   Includes index.
   ISBN 0-8120-4413-4
   1. Public relations. I. Title. II. Series.
HD59.D68 1990
659—dc20   90-37819

PRINTED IN ITALY

5 6 7 8   9929   7 6 5 4 3 2

Preface

Are you ever envious when you see other companies and their products mentioned in the media? Here's good news. You can compete for that space and time. Don't knock them. Join them.

This book has been written to build your business, not your ego. It concentrates on publicity with a purpose:

- to make your product or company better known
- to increase product sales
- to open new market segments
- to pre-sell the real decision makers
- to change or improve your company or product image

If you own a small business or hold a managerial position with a large company, whether you handle the publicity yourself or direct a staff of experts, this book is for you. It will teach you what publicity is, how it works, and how to design the best program for your publicity needs. You will also learn how to spot news in your company, write a news release, and how to back up your publicity with photographs.

If the media—and how to get free publicity in it—is a mystery to you now, it won't be after you study this book. You will learn all you need to know about the consumer and business-to-business press, as well as television and radio. How to deal with the press is also covered to help when you:

- face a business crisis
- stage a special event
- hold a press conference

John Diggs, a fictitious businessperson employed to help demonstrate each point, will always be available to guide you every step of the way until you reach each goal.

Now it's your turn to make someone jealous. Good luck!

DOROTHY I. DOTY

Contents

What Publicity Is

INTRODUCTION AND MAIN POINTS

In this chapter we will introduce you to the practice of business publicity, as well as how and why it has become so important to the health and welfare of life and business today. We will focus on the similarities between news reporting and publicity and on the special working relationship between a business and the media.

After studying the material in this chapter:

■ You will learn the history and importance of business news.

■ You will get a "feel" for what is news and what is not news.

■ You will understand the necessity of reporting your news.

■ You will begin to understand your role as a reporter.

■ You will learn how to work effectively with the media.

■ You will learn how to study the media to effectively use it. to promote your business, your products, and your services.

In the old days, a newspaper editor or reporter would walk down Main Street, poke his head in each store and ask, "Any news today?"

The proprietor of the general store might respond, "Tell the ladies that I've just received a shipment of new dress fabrics from New York!"

The restaurant owner might report, "Our new stove just arrived. Tell the folks we can serve them faster now."

The dressmaker might say, "I just finished a new dress for Jane Winston. She has company coming next week."

And a farmer, in town for the day on business, might stop in at the newspaper office and report, "I just bought that stretch of land down there by the river."

It was a fair trade: the business person got free publicity; the newspaper got news. It is no less true today.

Over time, business news itself has changed very little. Business today still has its new products, companies buy new equipment, the service industry still reports on the services it performs, and businesses continue to expand. And of course there is always "people news."

But can you imagine a reporter or editor today stopping by your office and asking, "Any news today?"

BUSINESS PUBLICITY IS THE LONG ARM OF JOURNALISM

Throughout the world people are fascinated by the news of business. No wonder. It hits us where we live—and where we work. We are, after all, engaged in the daily struggle for economic survival. This intense interest we have in business news developed during the Great Depression of the 1930s when one's very existence depended not only on the local economy but on the nation's economy as well.

Today, newspapers all over the country—indeed, all over the world—have pages and sometimes sections packed with business news; television and radio stations have entire programs or segments of programs devoted to business news; and there are myriad trade, industrial, and professional journals that report only business news. Where does it all come from?

Obviously, there aren't enough reporters and editors to gather the news themselves, so who does report it? You do—and business people like you.

A lot of business news still originates with the media, but over the past several decades each company has become more and more responsible for the reporting of its own business news. This is called *publicity*.

Remember: news is news—regardless of who reports it.

YOU PROVIDE A SERVICE WHEN YOU SEND A NEWS RELEASE

You are not asking a favor when you provide a legitimate business news story. I stress this because for a long time publicity got a bad rap. It was thought that for any business to be mentioned in the press, you had to practically beg for it. Even publicity people believed this.

Of course, there were some (publicists) who, true enough, relied on favors instead of coming up with solid news stories. I suppose there are some still around. I hope you won't be among them, especially since it is so simple to find and provide hard business news to the media.

EDITORS OFTEN RELY ON PUBLICITY RELEASES TO MAKE ASSIGNMENTS

Reporting the business news—your business news—is your responsibility. Journalists rarely "stumble on" a story. In most cases they are assigned a story. When you send in a news release or memo or when you call the city desk, you alert the city editor to the story in your business. Whether or not a good news story is printed, however, depends to a large extent upon the importance of the news you provide, as well as the competition for the editorial space by other news sources: local, national, and international.

THE BEAT REPORTER HAS BECOME A SPECIALIST

The original reporter covered the Main Street "beat." Today the beat reporter is usually found only in small towns and suburban areas. Modern business has become so complex and technological advances have contributed to such rapid change in almost every industry that reporters found it impossible to know everything about everything. Beat reporters began to specialize. Now they are often known as business news specialists. Has this solved the problem? No, not really. It is still impossible for the specialist to know everything about everything, even in a single industry. This brings us to you and your business.

THINK OF YOURSELF AS *YOUR* BUSINESS NEWS SPECIALIST

There is no one—not a business reporter or specialist—who knows as much about your business as you do. When it comes to your business, you are the expert. Indeed, you are so plugged into your business that unlike the specialist, you know in advance when news will break. You know well ahead of time about the purchase of new equipment, the hiring of new personnel, even acquisitions and mergers. Why wouldn't you be in a better position to report the news of your company than any media specialist?

Moreover, you know the most intimate details of any and every bit of news generated by your company. This is no small advantage.

AS A BUSINESS PERSON, YOU ARE A VALUABLE NEWS SOURCE

A reporter is responsible for developing a friendly relationship with and establishing communications with key business people in the community or industry. This is where you come in. You are the reporter's best source of information about your company and your industry.

Since your business is so intimately involved with the industry as a whole, you are alert to industrial and economic trends in the field. You know and understand the details of the commodity and its production. In fact, you are in the perfect position to educate the media about the industry and its importance to the economy of the community, the state, perhaps even the nation.

You Know More About Your Retail Store

If your business is a retail store, the media can look to you for news about changes in working hours, wages, and working conditions. You can keep them informed about plans for expansion, planned renovations for the physical plant, or expansions in service or new lines of products being carried by your store. The media also depend on you to report changes in both wholesale and retail prices, especially when they are part of an important local or national trend.

In addition, there are always the personal items about the store clerks, the department managers, and yourself, the owner; trips taken by store executives and their buying excursions; promotions and changes in personnel. All these topics are but a few of the possibilities for story coverage on the retail level.

You Know More About Your Real Estate Firm

The transactions of any real estate firm are news. In your position you may know about the sale and acquisition of business and residential property in your community. You may have the details on the real estate involved and the new uses to which it is being put. You know about new construction, new buildings, and new residences.

This information is more valuable than the mere listing of facts. It reveals much about new businesses coming into the community and about the expansion in old businesses. In fact, real estate news has become such a vital factor today that most larger newspapers have set aside special pages or even entire sections devoted solely to real estate.

You Know More About Your Manufacturing or Wholesale Business

If yours is a manufacturing or wholesale business, your company has the same news elements as the retail store—and then some. You are the media source for new research information, new processes, new machines, and certainly new technology.

Also, through your manufacturing or wholesale establishment, you may keep in touch with important local industries or with major commodity producers, placing you in the position to give the media an overall picture of business in your community. Your company may even become for the media the barometer for an entire region.

You Know More About Your New Product

New products are being launched every day. This is not news. What is news is the specific product that is new—your new product. Only you know the technology, the thinking, and the planning that went into your new product. Only you know your marketing and distribution plans. Only you know how it fits into the daily life of the individual, the community, perhaps even the nation. The reporter who covers new products needs you to supply this information.

YOU ARE A LOCAL SOURCE OF INFORMATION FOR THE TRADE

Trade journals and industrywide publications could not exist if it were not for people like you. Unless you continually feed them the news about your businesses, there would be no news reported at all. They depend on you for technical information, educational material, news, general stories, and feature material.

Business papers cover changes of ownership, new and improved products, inventions and developments, and the construction of new plants, as well as the more personal side of your business—news about individuals in your business or industry.

The trade and industrial press is vitally important not only to the industry it covers, but to the local and national media as well. To reporters and specialists, these are the "bibles" of the industry. When a story is of particular significance, a trade publication may even send proofs of important articles to the newspapers and magazines of more general circulation. Can you think of a better reason for keeping the trades supplied with information about your business?

THE NEWS YOU CREATE

The need for this section became apparent as I spoke with business men and women about publicity and how their companies use it. My interpretation of the word *publicity* and their understanding of what it entailed were so far apart that I feel a need to clarify the term so that we are all talking the same language.

During the course of my conversations, one man had told me that his company had a brochure. Then he added, "I don't even like to give it out because it doesn't cover any of the points I feel should be covered."

"We have a tour of our factory," volunteered a woman in the group.

Another responded, "We do a lot of advertising in the trade journals."

Someone in retailing spoke up: "One time we had a man dress as a gorilla to amuse the kids."

Technically, all these people are on the right track. Webster has defined publicity as "Any information or action that brings a person, cause, etc. to public notice"; consequently, these must all be considered aspects of publicity.

SPECIAL EVENTS MUST BE REPORTED TO BE PUBLICITY

For the purposes of this book, a sales promotion, special event, advertising, and other created news is simply a promotion until it is reported. A special event, for example, becomes publicity for your business only when the news of its happening appears in the media, just as new equipment for your plant becomes publicity only when it is reported. Special events in this sense are a means to publicity, not publicity itself.

■ For example, a paid advertisement is clearly not, in our sense, publicity. However, if you announce to the business editor that you have developed a new advertising campaign, giving the theme and anything interesting about it, and if that editor mentions your new advertising campaign in the newspaper or on television or radio, this is publicity.

■ A brochure is not publicity. It is considered sales promotion, but if your trade journal reports that your company is offering a new brochure, this is publicity.

■ A tour of your factory is not publicity, even though it may be excellent public relations. However, if a newspaper reporter takes the tour and writes it up for her paper, if a television station sends a cameraman along to record the tour as a public service educational feature, if someone newsworthy (a local dignitary or visiting celebrity) takes the tour and this is reported by the media, this is publicity.

■ A man dressed up as a gorilla to amuse the children is promotion. However, if the press reports that the gorilla will be at your place of business or if you have the gorilla doing something unusual, like climbing the side of a building, then this becomes news and the media will probably cover the event. The result, again, is publicity.

IS PUBLICITY FREE?

Not entirely. Publicity is free only in the sense that you are not required to pay for the space in the press or for time on television or radio. The reason is that publicity is, or should be, news and, as such, appears in the news or editorial columns or airtime of the media. You provide editors with something they need. You give them news, and the media do not charge for reporting the news.

DOES YOUR ADVERTISING DOLLAR ENTITLE YOU TO "FREE" PUBLICITY?

It would be naive to say that an advertiser has absolutely no influence on the editorial department of the media. Indeed, an advertiser often has considerable influence since the media are businesses, like any other business, with a "bottom line." Therefore, giving an advertiser free time or space may be considered a means of attracting more business.

It's often true that your "news" angle may not need to be as strong as that of a non-advertiser; in some cases, you may be able to get away with a purely promotional pitch if your company is a heavy advertiser in that particular medium or if that medium would like you to be.

When a company asks its advertising representative to "get us a story" in the paper or to get someone from your company on that television or radio show, however, this has a decidedly chilling effect on any reputable media person or on a public relations person.

The fact is, if you really put your mind to it, in most cases you will be able to come up with a news angle that will often make you welcome, advertiser or not. If you want to be respected in this profession, I suggest that you not trade on your advertising dollar.

BEGIN YOUR PUBLICITY CAMPAIGN BY DOING YOUR HOMEWORK

The media are your textbooks. Instead of passively reading the newspaper and trade publications, watching television, or listening to radio, concentrate on what you read, see, or hear. Try to figure out why a particular story was reported. Was a business or product mentioned? Why? How did they mention it without making it sound like a "plug" for an advertiser. How can you tell it is publicity, not advertising?

Become alert to what other companies are reporting and how they report it. Become as familiar with the interests and needs of the media as you are with those of your company.

CHAPTER PERSPECTIVE

This chapter gave you a sense of responsibility toward the media as well as toward your own business and its products and services. This book will continue to stress the importance of dealing only in legitimate business news and explain how to report that news in a professional manner. In addition, it will present the professional ways and means of doing this.

Cutting Publicity Down To Your Size

CHAPTER 2

INTRODUCTION AND MAIN POINTS

In this chapter we will explain how to set your publicity goals and why it is important to do so. We will help you focus on the specific publicity needs of your company, your products, and your service.

After studying the material in this chapter:

▬ You will be able to set your publicity objectives.

▬ You will be able to trim your publicity to fit your geographical needs.

▬ You will be able to cut your publicity down to reach and concentrate only on your potential buyers.

▬ You will be able to cut your publicity down to available human resources.

▬ You will be able to cut your publicity down to the time you have available to devote to publicity.

▬ You will be able to cut your publicity down to the money you can afford to spend on publicity.

▬ You will be able to concentrate on the media that reaches your specific buying public.

▬ You will be able to cut your publicity down to specific consumer, trade, technical, professional, or farm markets and the publications that reach these markets.

The manager of a small office nearby recently told me she planned to quit her job. What she really wanted to do, she said, was decorate and sell cakes. This was something she really enjoyed, something she was trained to do.

Naturally this triggered my publicity reflexes, and growing excited about her publicity possibilities, I began telling her how she could get stories in the newspapers, get on television and radio . . . I went on and on.

Suddenly I realized I had lost my audience. She drew away from me in horror. Instead of helping her, I had frightened her.

Cake decorating she knew; publicity was unknown territory. Finally I said, "Look, all you really need to get started in business is a story in your local newspaper. I'll help you write it."

Her face brightened. I got my audience back.

Thinking about this later, I recalled what Agatha Christie's famous detective, Hercules Poirot, said: "One should not need to use a rapier to cut the string of a parcel."

A SIZE YOU CAN HANDLE

Cutting your publicity down to your size simply means being realistic about what you need as well as how much you can handle. I mean this from an emotional as well as a practical point of view.

The lady who decorates cakes might have gotten a lot of publicity, but emotionally she wasn't ready for it. Also, she instinctively knew that she really didn't need so much publicity, that it would be a waste of time, money, and effort.

If you get an anxiety attack just thinking about having to get publicity for someone or something, especially when you read about all the publicity you could be getting, you are not alone. After all these years in the business, I am still overwhelmed by the possibilities.

On the other hand, your head might be spinning with ideas, but you don't have the time, the energy, or perhaps the human resources necessary to do it all. The opportunities for publicity are so vast that if you don't learn how to cut publicity down to your size, you will give up before you even get started.

Don't stop reading now. Let's cut your publicity down to size—the size you, your product, your service, your project, or your company needs—a size you know you can handle. We'll take the most obvious areas first.

HOW MUCH PUBLICITY IS REALISTIC—FOR YOU?

Few entrepreneurs are shy about getting publicity. Most want a lot of it. They expect stories in newspapers all over the country, interviews on national television and radio, and stories in the trade, professional, or technical journals. And that's just the first week.

There is, of course, the really big thinker who expects a story in *Fortune*—next month! The reasoning goes something like this: "If IBM can get an article in *Fortune*, why can't we?" This sort of reasoning can drive a publicist mad.

Now, don't get me wrong. I'm not saying it can't be done. Obviously, there is always the possibility of getting a publicity story in any media—national as well as local. If you think you can do it, good luck. After all, it's the mark of a winner to think big.

However, if you expect this sort of publicity on your maiden voyage, your self-confidence must be staggering. I suspect you've got a cache of press agents hidden somewhere, or a potential news story the likes of which is rarely seen in the business world.

Most of us would think twice before tackling such a gargantuan task. The labor hours alone would be prohibitive even for a professional staff and virtually impossible for anyone working alone.

YOUR HUMAN RESOURCES

There is a tendency in all of us to think: if it's free, grab it. The most common mistake beginning publicists make is to try to get any publicity anyplace, without discretion or any goal in mind.

Indeed, there are so many publicity possibilities for any company, product, service, or project that they could keep you and an entire staff busy twenty-four hours a day, seven days a week, just checking them all out, and then you would realize to your dismay that you still missed many opportunities.

Do you really have the help necessary to get publicity just for the sake of taking advantage of "free" time or space? Few companies do. Before setting your publicity goals, consider just how many people you can afford to commit to the project. You can only spread yourself, and your other human resources, so far.

"Human resources" implies more than the staff necessary to write the stories and contact the media. Keep in mind that not everyone is qualified to speak for the company, whether that company is simply you and your business, or a large corporation.

The appropriate people must be available to appear on television and radio interviews, someone credible to be quoted in the media on subjects of substance. This generally means an executive with the company—anyone from the chief executive officer on down. It means taking someone in a critical position away from his or her first-line work and responsibilities. If it is your company and you are trying to build a fledging business, it means taking you away from some other job critical to running the business itself.

How much of this can you do all by yourself? Do you have a staff large enough to take care of all these things? If not, cut back on the amount of publicity until your staff of assistants grows to fit your needs.

Here are a few things you can do to trim your publicity to fit your human resources:

▪ Use query letters to all editors before submitting a story. Give them the basic information, along with your credentials or the credentials of your sources, so that you don't spend time writing a story that won't be accepted.

▪ If you don't have a good writer, stick to television and radio interviews.

▪ If you have a Personal Computer, learn to use all of its potential functions. (See Chapter 5.)

▪ If you don't have an adequate staff to turn out mass mailings, stick to exclusive stories you can manage yourself.

▪ Not all business executives are great for television and radio interviews. You may be a great business person but feel uncomfortable before a camera or microphone. Don't fret. If appropriate personalities are not available to appear on television and radio interviews, stick to news and magazine stories.

▪ Before you arrange for any executive media interviews, obtain the fixed travel and appointment schedules of the executives in question so that you can utilize their time and yours to obtain the best possible coverage in the least possible time.

▪ Before you interview someone for background information and for quotes that can be extracted for use in the print media, plan to gather all the information you need in one sitting.

▪ Do your homework. Study the biography of the person you are to interview so you can limit your questions to his or her area of expertise.

■ Write a set of questions for which you know you need answers before you go any further. Get these out of the way first.

■ Anticipate questions the media will ask. If you are focusing on a specific business problem or crisis, ask the hard questions. Try to get some straight answers.

■ Tape each interview, and have it transcribed immediately. If there are any further questions to be answered before you can get on with your work, now is the time to clarify them. If you can't get more time with the subject, write additional questions and submit them.

■ Make maximum use of those human resources you do have. For instance, the CEO is not the only person in a company whom it is interesting to interview. Consider the technicians, inventors, and engineers, or even someone who has been with the company for a long time and has interesting anecdotes to relate.

■ If you don't have enough people on your staff to write news releases, take photographs, and contact the media, look around your company and among your friends and family for those who might volunteer their services. It's amazing how many people like to get involved in publicity. Let them.

■ Tie in with special events in your community to take advantage of the publicity personnel already working on a project.

AVAILABLE TIME

Publicity absorbs time like a sponge. Don't let it overtake you as well. The fact is, publicity is sneaky. Sometimes it seems to take on a life of its own. You begin with one television or newspaper interview. First, there's the preparation: a biography to prepare, some background material on your business, letters to send and confirm, pictures to take . . . well, you get the idea. You may not need all these, but you must be prepared to supply them to the media if they are requested. In the meantime, who's minding the store? Who's decorating the cakes?

If you are just starting a new business, consider how much time you can afford to take away from the running of the business itself. If your company is large, you need to consider the time of those who will represent your company. Your goals and your publicity plans must accommodate the time the appointed person can afford to give you.

Don't take on too much until you know you can handle it from a personal and practical point of view. Let me give you a rough idea of the time it takes to get publicity. It takes time to make telephone calls to "sell" the media on a story or interview. It takes time to research and write a story. It takes time to come up with publicity ideas and special events.

You need time to get across town to a television interview, and then time to wait. You need travel time to different cities where you have scheduled interviews or special promotions.

There are ways you can manage your time more effectively and thereby cut down on the time necessary to get publicity:

■Focus on your goals, and learn to say "no" if the project doesn't advance your specific interests.

■Prepare fact sheets and biographies, take photographs, and organize and prepare everything you can before making your contacts.

■Provide the media with all the details, facts, and technical information the first time around so you don't have to spend additional time going over the same route the second time.

■Plan only one thing at a time, and follow it to completion before you begin something else.

■Schedule so there are no conflicts in time or preparation that require additional calls and arrangements.

■Schedule only what you know you can handle.

■Tie in with other projects for which someone else is handling the details.

THE SIZE OF YOUR POCKETBOOK

People often refer to "free" publicity, and certainly publicity is less expensive than advertising, sales promotion, or even a sales call. Don't kid yourself, however. The only thing really free about publicity is that you don't pay for space in the print media or time on television or radio. If you must pay for it, for example a mention on a quiz show, it falls into the category of sales promotion or advertising. For our purposes we don't call this publicity.

For a large company, the expenses involved in publicity are often considered minimal and are easily absorbed. Even with the largest company, however, it is always wise to plan a publicity budget and try to stay within it. Someone, someday, will hold you to an accounting.

In a small, struggling, or new business, pennies count. If you're not careful, you may run out of cash before you run into new customers. You don't want to be a victim of the adage, "The operation was a success but the patient died." You don't want a lot of publicity but a dead business on your hands.

■ Make your advance preparations so that you don't need costly emergency services to get you out of a scrape.

■ Shop around for the best prices in everything you use and do.

■ Study the media you plan to contact. Clip stories similar to those you expect to send in as news releases. Use these as guides for your own news releases.

■ Learn to do as much of the writing yourself as possible. Taking a journalism class might be a good investment in both time and money.

■ Send your news releases only to those media you know are interested in the subject.

■ Send your news releases well in advance of the release date so you do not incur extra postage charges.

CONCENTRATE ONLY ON PUBLICITY THAT CAN BENEFIT YOUR BUSINESS

Publicity can be pretty heady stuff. If a neighbor or friend sees you on television or reads about you in the newspaper, it means instant status. What is your first reaction? Most of us want more of the same. Does it sell more product? Who cares? It's great for the ego. This euphoria lasts until the end of the month, perhaps, or maybe even until the end of the quarter when you are forced to look at the bottom line: disaster!

While you have been out getting famous for fifteen minutes, nobody has been minding the store. While you were becoming a celebrity, your business, your product, or your service may have profited very little—perhaps not at all. You may have spent hours, days, or even months getting your name or your company's name in the media, only to discover that it all adds up to nothing: no increase in sales, no improvement in the company image—nothing. When it comes to business, this sort of publicity just doesn't pay.

SET YOUR PUBLICITY OBJECTIVES

It's true that thinking too small about publicity can be just as unrealistic as thinking too big, but why waste time on something that doesn't pay off in an important way for your company, your product, or your service? One way you can keep your perspective about publicity is to ask yourself this question: "Would I *buy* advertising time or space in this medium?" When it comes to spending hard earned cash for advertising, one can get mighty practical. Try to be just as practical about your publicity.

Being practical about your publicity really comes down to setting publicity objectives to reach specific business goals. Maybe you need only a little local publicity. On the other hand, if you face a business crisis, you may need to pull out all the stops. Determining just what it is you want to accomplish is the first task of a publicist.

Say you decide to call in a publicity expert. What would that expert do? My first questions to you are, Why publicity now? What has happened to trigger this sudden need for publicity? You must be able to answer these questions before we can get started. Maybe you're just going into business and want as many people as possible to know that you and your new company exist. Perhaps your company has an important anniversary coming up and the boss wants lots of news coverage. The possible reasons are numerous. The following questions may give you an idea of some of the more common objectives:

■Are you starting a new business and looking for your first few customers?

■Are you introducing a new product or service?

■Does your company, product, or service need to be better known?

■Are you moving to a new location and need to inform your buying public?

■Is your company about to celebrate an important anniversary?

■Do you want to promote a special event?

■Are you specifically interested in getting a large turnout for a parade or a special holiday event?

■ Do you need to expand the use of your product?

■ Do you need to educate your customers in the proper use of your product?

■ Do you want to stimulate inquiries and requests?

■ Do you want to expand your present market?

■ Do you need to identify and locate potential new customers?

■ Do you need to reach your real decision makers?

■ Do you need to pave the way for your sales representatives by announcing your product?

■ Do you need to cut down on the number of "service" or "courtesy" calls necessary to maintain good relations with your accounts?

■ Does your product or company image need to be improved?

■ Do you need to build a better reputation for your company and its products or services?

■ Do you have a serious or potentially serious business problem or crisis that publicity can help you solve?

■ Are sales sagging in a specific region?

Your business problem, whatever it may be, is as unique as your business. By pinpointing the reason you need publicity at this particular moment, you establish your goals and automatically eliminate a lot of work.

Now, let's tailor your publicity so that it fits this need without excess effort or time.

FOCUS YOUR PUBLICITY ON SPECIFIC AREAS OF GEOGRAPHIC NEED

In *The New York Times* recently, there was a small story about a cake decorator in Taiwan. The headline read, "Your Father's Face on a Cake." Now what possible good could this story in a New York newspaper do a baker in Taiwan? Would you order a cake from Taiwan, even with your father's face on it?

It's obvious even to the amateur that if your sales are sagging in the South, it is foolish to spend valuable time trying to get publicity in the West. There are other areas of geographic need, however, that aren't quite so obvious.

Every product or service has its own natural boundaries. These boundaries may be determined by the area in which the business is located, by where the product is distributed, or by a sales territory. These boundaries may be determined by where your potential customers live: inland or on the coast, in the mountains or in the desert, in the cities or in rural areas. They may be determined by climate: hot or cold, rainy or dry. These boundaries may be local, regional, national, or international.

It's likely that you need more than a story in your local newspaper, but do you really need all the media blitz of the nation's bicentennial? Don't laugh. Some beginners, and all too many clients, think like this. Not many people today blanch when they think of getting publicity.

If you decide, "Of course, we don't need national publicity—we're a local business," then the next step is to limit your publicity goals to the local media. If your business covers an entire region or a section of the country, you should of course expand your publicity expectations and plans to cover the same territory that your business covers.

If at any time in the near future you plan to expand the distribution and sales of your product into other sales territories, some "teaser" publicity in those areas would not be amiss.

Most publicity outside your product's natural boundaries is wasted. Generally speaking, if your business comes only from your neighborhood or hometown, then this is where you should concentrate your publicity efforts. If you draw business from throughout the state or region, then your publicity should be restricted to this territory.

▬Confer with your sales department to clearly define the problem area that needs the most publicity—right now. It may be a single sales territory where a salesperson needs support, perhaps against a competitor.

▬If you are introducing a new product or service, cooperate with your marketing department to back up its local, regional, or national product introduction coverage with appropriate media publicity. For example, if your company is introducing a new product in Chicago, concentrate your publicity in the Chicago area.

▬When your advertising department plans a new ad campaign, gear your publicity to back it up and expand its effectiveness in those areas where it will be seen. Select the media for their geographic reach.

Markets were once segmented only by geography simply because the state of transportation and communications required salespeople to concentrate on those geographic areas they could reach in one or two days. Although geography is still important, it isn't the sole factor in sales, advertising, marketing, or even publicity.

Each product or service, each business, has its own buying public as well. Which is yours: teenagers, young marrieds, florists, farmers, chemists, engineers? Suddenly, simply by answering this question, you have zeroed in on your buying public. You have automatically cut down on the amount of publicity you need and the places where you need to get it. What a savings you have already made!

Whether your product is aimed at the consumer market, the industrial market, or the farm market, your buying public is still comprised of individuals, individuals who read and who often learn about your product only through the various forms of communication that are edited specifically for them.

By identifying your buyers and concentrating on reaching only them, you have trimmed your publicity to the most productive size for your needs.

Your Potential Buying Public

No matter what your product may be, you face the problem not of reaching the general public, but of reaching your potential buyers. Always remember when planning your publicity and when writing your news releases that you are not speaking to a mass of people melded together into some amorphous unrecognizable block.

The people you address are individuals like yourself who have jobs to do, paychecks to earn, and families to support. Yet each is different. What makes one group into a "market segment" is a similar interest: job specification, education or lack of it, age, marital status, whether or not they are in school, and anything else that makes them unique.

The closer you can pinpoint these special qualities and similar interests, the more directly and personally you can speak to your particular market.

If your product sells only to teenagers, why would you even bother trying to reach and "sell" senior citizens? If your product isn't for teenagers, then who is your customer, your potential customer? Do you make toys for toddlers? Do you want to reach the "thirtysomething" crowd?

Of course, if your product is for toddlers, your market is defined not only by the age of the child but also by the child-rearing interests of the parents, and so are your publicity possibilities.

A Special Interest

If you sell auto supplies, you need customers who own cars. If you sell products for pets, you need to reach pet owners. Just think of all the special-interest groups out there: science, retirement, travel, camping and trailers, photography, art, astrology, aviation, the environment, education, skiing, soccer, swimming, golf—well, you get the idea. Certainly you know to what special-interest group your product or service should be targeted, and as you undoubtedly also know, each interest group has its own special-interest publications in addition to the general media.

However, it is possible that your product or service may be adapted to more than one interest group, perhaps many. It may be that there are more potential interest groups out there than you ever imagined. Obviously you should never lock yourself in, but to keep aiming in the dark over and over again is wasteful:

■Make a concerted effort to identify those interest groups who are potential buyers, and then target your publicity to those particular groups—and only those.

■Study the specific publications that print your type of product news, and write your news releases in their particular style.

From the following list of market segments, select the one you wish to reach right now. Actually, you can check off those several you wish to reach ultimately, but it is wise to deal with only one at a time.

CONSUMER MARKETS
By age group
■Young children

— Teenagers
— Young adults
— Mature or middle-aged
— Senior citizens

By educational status
— Just starting school
— Grade school education
— High school education
— College or university education
— Individuals holding graduate degrees

By financial status and interests
— Low income
— Middle income
— High income
— Wealthy

Other consumer market segments can be broken down by social status, cultural background and heritage, cultural interests, recreational interests, sex, social class, personality attributes, marital status, and presence and age of children.

Those with Similar Occupations

Suppose you manufacture an industrial product. Does it really do you any good to get on a television interview show, even a big, national show, in the middle of the day? Who sees it? Do your potential buyers see it? Probably not. First, they're probably at work—buying. Second, it's probably not the sort of show they would watch, anyway.

What about a story in your local newspaper, even a front-page story? Great, right? What if your buyer lives in the next town or another state?

What's left? It may not be very glamorous, and your neighbors probably won't be impressed, but what about a story in the trade publication that serves the industry that uses your type of product? Bingo! Suddenly, you've hit on the one medium that reaches all your potential buyers in one fell swoop. By adding more facts than you could ever get into a general news story, you give them the buying information they need to make a decision. And it takes so little time and effort!

How can you get a list of trade publications in your field? There are several methods. Some public libraries maintain a list of trade and professional publications to which they subscribe. From this list, which will be categorized by trade or profession, you can request publications by name and date of publication. Colleges and universities often have trade publications for reference also.

Your library also will probably have directories of trade publications—national and international—which will give you a detailed media list in almost any field that might be of interest to you.

In the library, or in your local bookstore, you can get a copy of the *Writer's Market*, which lists publications for many different trade, professional and technical interests. And your own advertising department or agency might have a copy of the *Standard Rate & Data.*

▬Each industry has its own "bible." This is the publication that everyone in the business must read to keep abreast of that particular industry. Instead of sending out general news releases to half a dozen or more, take the time to carefully study the specific publication, see what sort of news is printed, and note how many facts and how much detail is required for a story to get a reasonable amount of space.

▬Armed with this information, locate the person in the company who can give you this sort of technical and detailed information.

▬Alert selected executives and technicians to your quest for news about new developments and discoveries. Ask them to contact you immediately when there is anything to report.

▬Give credit where credit is due. This is a good way to keep the sources of news actively looking for new developments to report to you.

▬If there is a professional in your company who can write an article for a trade, technical, or professional publication in his or her field, contact the appropriate publication to see if you can get them an assignment. In this way you get a valuable article in a trade publication that can directly affect your sales, yet *you* need not invest the time in writing the article.

▬Suggest an article idea to the editor of a specific trade publication in your field. If the editor likes your suggestion, a free-lance writer in your area can be given the assignment. This writer is an excellent contact for future articles as well.

▬Try to find out the names of other free-lance writers in your area, individuals who welcome suggestions for current and future stories they can sell to trade publications in your field.

If possible, get to know the editors of the publications directly related to your company's business and its products and services. In this way you keep ahead of the publicity pack.

Familiarize yourself with the special columns and regular features in each magazine. You may be able to get publicity for your company, product, or service merely with a one-line column note in a widely read publication.

THE APPROPRIATE MEDIA

When you want to meet someone special, you go where you know that person will be. A shotgun approach to publicity is wasteful. If you haven't done it already, some research is in order. You may get lucky and hit the target; it is more likely that you will be way off base. Scattered shots mean wasted ammunition.

An important part of cutting your publicity down to your size is trimming the choice of media. This not only saves time and effort but it saves money as well.

In analyzing the media that reach your present and potential customers, consider whether these customers are more inclined to read the newspapers (local or large metropolitan newspapers), watch television (news, sports, talk shows, and variety shows), listen to radio (news, talk shows, or music stations), or read special-interest publications (consumer or trade).

Study the media you intend to use. Make sure they use the sort of story you are sending, or change your release to fit their format.

Determine the territory you need to cover. Do you really need publicity all over the country? No? Then omit wire services, national consumer publications, and national television for the time being. What about publicity outside your region or your state? No? Then you can eliminate a mass mailing of press releases to statewide and regional news media.

Keep your list of publications up to date. Don't waste time and money sending queries and articles to publications that are no longer in business.

CHAPTER PERSPECTIVE

This chapter helped you to pinpoint your immediate publicity goal(s) to cut your publicity down to size and to simplify the next task of planning your publicity program and selecting the media on which you need to concentrate to reach your goals.

How To Plan Your Publicity Campaign

INTRODUCTION AND MAIN POINTS

In this chapter we will assist you in creating a workable publicity plan specifically for your business, product, or service. You will learn why a plan is necessary to keep you on track in order to avoid wasting time and money. You will also build on the goals you formed in the previous chapter.

After studying the material in this chapter:

■ You will learn how and where to collect the historical and biographical information needed to plan an effective program.

■ You will see how your company's locale affects your publicity planning.

■ You will see the importance of creating a company calendar of past, as well as current, events.

■ You will learn how to search out the new and interesting in both the front office and "backstage."

■ You will learn how to interview key people, including "old-timers" and outsiders, for publicity possibilities.

■ You will understand the types and importance of photographs.

■ You will learn how to generate publicity ideas.

■ You will get samples of one-of-a-kind publicity programs.

Recently I had the following conversation with the owner of a delicatessen in Queens, New York. He said "All I want to know is, how can I get publicity?"

"Where do you want this publicity," I asked. "Where do you need it?"

He shrugged his shoulders: "Anywhere I can get it."

"How about Osage City, Kansas?" I asked.

"Of course not," he said.

"In Miami, Florida? Would publicity in Miami do you any good? Would people who live in Miami come to your deli in Queens?"

"No, I guess not," he admitted.

"Then," I said, "you want your publicity to reach your potential customers, right?"

"Right," he responded. "That means publicity only in this neighborhood?"

"Do all of your customers come from this neighborhood?" I asked.

"No. I get a lot of truckers coming off the Long Island Expressway. They stop here for coffee in the mornings."

"Is this the first deli they pass when they get off the expressway?"

He shook his head thoughtfully for a moment, then said; "No. Actually, they would pass five or six delis before they get to mine."

"Why do they wait until they get to your deli before stopping for coffee?" I persisted.

"I asked a guy that once. He said that here he could always find a place to park."

Within a few minutes and after a little thought, this deli owner had set a goal: to build traffic. He had identified two important market segments: those living in the neighborhood and the truckers from the Long Island Expressway. He had also discovered at least one sales message: "You'll be able to find a parking space."

He had started to plan his publicity program. He wouldn't call it that, of course, but that's what it was—a plan to direct his publicity efforts, a plan tailored to his needs.

The size of the publicity program necessary for your company might be larger geographically, or it might be larger in concept. The basic point remains the same: tailor your plan to meet your company's publicity or public relation needs.

WHY IS A PUBLICITY PLAN NECESSARY?

Without a written plan, publicity tends to take on a life of its own. You make one telephone call, and suddenly a chain reaction takes over.

You set up a television interview for the client. The television contact requests a biography of the client, some information about the company, the product, or the service, and perhaps some photographs. You collect and send them. This takes time. You must get them out before you can set up a newspaper interview.

Then you take the client to the television station—someone always accompanies the client to an interview—and another afternoon is shot.

The client gets a kick out of being interviewed on television. He is suddenly a celebrity among his friends and neighbors. He indicates that he'd like more of the same. He doesn't actually come right out and admit it. What he says is, "I think this is the sort of thing that will really increase our business." Down deep inside, you don't believe this, but after all he is the client and he's paying the bills. So you set up more television interviews.

On the way to yet another television show, the client asks what happened to that newspaper interview you promised. What do you do, make excuses? Blame the delay on him? No, you call the editor that afternoon. The editor wants a biography and photographs. He also wants to interview the client at the very time the client is scheduled for another show. Since you are not about to tell an editor he comes in second, you make some plausible excuse and arrange for another time. There go your plans for writing that trade news release. You'll have to work late. And so it goes. The publicity campaign is totally out of control. Publicity has taken over. As Montaigne once wrote, "Once the ship gets underway, all the ropes start tugging."

IF EVERYONE IS HAPPY ABOUT THE PUBLICITY, WHY CHANGE?

Happy today is not necessarily happy tomorrow. The glamour of publicity eventually peters for even the most publicity-hungry clients when they realize that the store doesn't mind itself: if they don't get back to work, they won't have a store to get back to. When they get back to doing what they do best, you can get back to your plan.

I'm not saying that spontaneity, the unexpected, and the opportunity should be passed over. Indeed not. I'm only alerting you to the fact that in publicity there is always a day of reckoning. This usually arrives when someone checks the bottom line and asks, "Is publicity really worth it?" All too often the answer is "no."

A PUBLICITY PLAN HELPS YOU SET PRIORITIES

The goals or objectives that you establish won't do you a lick of good if you don't use them to help you set your publicity priorities on the day-to-day basis. Even when a massive amount of publicity is desirable, I have yet to see even the largest publicity firm have enough people, enough time, enough talent, or enough of anything to take advantage of all the publicity opportunities once a major publicity campaign is underway. When it comes to publicity, everything seems to happen at once.

Obviously, you, your boss, or your client can't be in a dozen places or be doing a dozen things at the same time. You must establish priorities. Something has to give way—yet how can you instantly determine which is more important?

A PUBLICITY PLAN KEEPS YOU ON TRACK

A publicity plan built around your objectives and goals not only gives you direction, it also keeps you on track. Remember the hazards of hit-or-miss publicity: a well-planned publicity program helps you make the important decisions and make them quickly. With a well-constructed program, your goal, as well as the means by which you intend to reach that goal, is constantly before you. It helps you know instantly when to say "yes" to a publicity project. If a project doesn't aim in the right direction, you simply say "no" and go on to some other project more in line with your objectives.

BEGIN WITH YOUR GOAL

Once you have your goal or goals, you pinpoint the methods—the route—by which you plan to reach these goals. Until you have the methods and means, your goal is simply a dream. How do you go about determining the means and methods of publicity when you hardly know what publicity is and certainly are unfamiliar with the methods and means available? Well, we are here to help you. First, however, you must contribute something from your end—the facts about your business, your products, and your services.

COLLECT THE FACTS

Before you can even think of planning your publicity or preparing a program, you must know precisely what tools you have. Facts are your basic publicity tools. You look for these facts everywhere from the front office to the shipping department, from your home office to the "outback," from your biggest customer to the smallest. This information won't just drop into your lap. You must look for it, perhaps even search high and low for it. How do you go about this?

Begin with the History of the Company

Even if your business is only one day old, it has a history. You have an anniversary—a start-up date. If your company is very old, it simply has a longer history.

Whether you created the company's history or others did it before you, don't rely on memory. Historical facts have a way of becoming obscured over time. You must dig them out.

You need dates, names, and facts of all sorts. Search the files for any previously written company history; dig up old newspaper stories that might have been printed along the way; pull out old letters, contracts, photographs—anything you can find about the company's background. Pay particular attention to unusual or interesting incidents about its beginnings, its growth, its changes, and its personnel over the years. You will probably be surprised at what you uncover—long-forgotten facts that might just make juicy tidbits for your publicity.

Examine the records for exact dates and precise facts related to important anniversaries. Comb the scrapbooks carefully for information that can be used for feature stories, column notes, and touchstones for special events.

Research Your Company's Financial History

Consider a financial history of the company. If your publicity plan is to encompass more than a new product introduction, a specific special event, or a limited publicity project, you may be called upon to provide a financial history of the company. At least be prepared. Get the facts, and write a business history of the company. In any event, prepare a fact sheet.

Accumulate Biographies of All Past and Present Principals

Make a complete list of every principal in or related to your company, along with their current titles. (It may save time later if you also obtain current addresses and telephone numbers.) Using this as a guide, collect biographical information on anyone you might use in your publicity program. Also make sure you have biographical data on anyone who has contributed significantly to your company's history. Begin with the founder, and work your way up to current executives, even major stockholders. Your company may have a library or "morgue" where this information can be located.

If several generations of one family have worked for the company over the years, make it a point to get biographies of all those individuals. Don't concentrate only on the bigwigs. If someone—anyone—has been with the company for a long time, get their personal history as well.

Get bios, too, of everyone directly connected with, for instance, your current special campaign. This includes such interesting professionals as the architect who designed your building and industrial designers who created your product, package, or trademark.

With luck, the people who founded and built your company may be an integral part of the history of your community. You can check the local library and historical society for some interesting background material. One of the most fascinating experiences I have had in collecting biographical data was when I planned a program for a large, national organization that was founded here in New York City. In going over the list of the founders, I recognized many names famous in New York's own history.

My first stop was the New York Historical Society—a perfect choice. All the names connected with the founding of the organization I was retained to publicize popped out at me from the history of the city itself. It was exciting, almost as if I were there myself. From the research I did in the Historical Society's library, I was able to collect enough historically rich facts and anecdotes to fill dozens of pages.

Most of this information ended up as column notes, "fillers" in newspapers and on television and radio shows all over the country. With each mention of the history of New York, the organization I was promoting was mentioned, too.

Your Company's Geographic Location May Be Significant

Your company may be sitting on an historical site—a possible publicity item. It may be housed in some historical building—another item.

The geographic location of your company is important in other terms, as well. For instance, no other company in the world is situated precisely where your company is situated; no other company in the world has the same location for its offices or distribution points; no other company in the world has precisely the same markets in precisely the same locations. The geographic facts about your company are unique. They are yours alone, and they are part of the information that will help you build a unique publicity program.

Would any other deli in the world, for instance, have the identical set of geographic circumstances as the one in Queens? Of course not. Although there were several other delis also right off the expressway, in each instance the surrounding neighborhood was different: different nationalities, different age segments, different religious organizations. All this information should be factored into a total publicity plan.

Keep in mind that if your business has more than one location, each should be examined for its geographic significance to your publicity program. Check out every single location.

This is also a reminder of the "neighborhood" you need to reach, whether it is a community, a state, a section of the country, the entire country—or perhaps even the world.

Make a Calendar of the Company's Anniversaries

In addition to the "red-letter days" on everyone's calendar—holidays and national anniversaries and events—every business has an individual calendar contour: annual events, anniversaries, and projects that are uniquely its own. These dates provide the framework around which a great deal of your company's publicity can be focused. Check your calendar regularly, and use these special occasions to get publicity. For example, you can time your publicity to coincide with the founding of the company, the birthday of its founder, and any recurring events you find in the company's past.

Take a Trip "Backstage"—Go Through the Plant

One of the first things I do when I begin working on a new account is to go behind the scenes. Usually this means taking a tour of the company's plant where the product is being manufactured or where the service is produced—perhaps the kitchen of a restaurant. It might also be a real backstage—of an opera, ballet, or theater. On these tours I can generally find ideas that can be demonstrated on television or written up as feature stories for newspapers. Also, I find that the enthusiasm generated by these tours spills over into my conversations with the media and helps "sell" them as well.

Before planning the publicity for a new household product, for instance, I was taken on a tour of the company's research laboratories where exciting things were happening. I spoke with the man who came up with the idea for the new product. He explained how it came about. He demonstrated the new product and used an older product, as well as a competitive product, to demonstrate the improvements and how the products differed. On many television shows they found this interesting enough that they let me use the same demonstration for their viewers. Indeed, this sort of backstage tour is so vital to your publicity program that you should insist that everyone working on a campaign take a guided tour through the plant.

What Is "Old Hat" to You May Be Exciting and New to Others

The common thread running through all my plant tours was that the things that were familiar and often dull to the people who worked there, were new and fascinating to me. And, as it turned out, they were fascinating to the media, their viewers and readers, as well.

If you are the owner, perhaps even the founder, of your company and nothing is new to you, consider enlisting fresh minds. Take someone totally unfamiliar with your company and product through the factory with you. You might consider a series of special public tours or educational tours for the express purpose of getting a fresh perspective. As the novice tours the plant with you, take special note of what it is that makes him stop and take a second look or ask questions. Encourage visitors to ask about anything that catches their attention. Take along a tape recorder so you have the questions, and your answers, on record. You'll be surprised at how much feature material you come up with. Look for anything that might make an interesting story.

Talk with the Key People

Make an inventory of the company's human resources. Meet and talk with as many key people—executives, designers, and plant superintendents—as possible, and learn what you can about their various responsibilities and departments. Obtain the benefit of their ideas and experience, and let them know you are open to publicity suggestions.

At the same time you can judge those who express themselves especially well and who have interesting anecdotes to share with the media. From these informal discussions and more formal interviews, you learn which of these people give the best interviews.

Don't Forget the Old-timers

Almost every company has at least one man or woman, perhaps someone who is retired, who remembers 'way back to the beginning—the beginning of the company, the beginning of the community, the beginning of something. These individuals can often provide you with a wealth of anecdotes. They often express themselves with such color that it is a good idea to tape any interviews or discussions you have with them. Spend some time with these old-timers, and you'll learn about the history of the company from an entirely different point of view.

Talk to People Who Make the Product

Your objectives and potential sources of problems come from the front office. When it's time for publicity ideas, though, go to the factory, the workshops, or their equivalent: the people who make the product, run the shops, and provide the services. Speak with as many employees as possible, especially those in the plants where the actual work is done. You'll be surprised how many interesting anecdotes you come up with.

Speak with "Outsiders" Who Are Involved in Current Projects

Whether your company has only one or many outside services, the individuals involved with those services, or even the service itself, might make interesting publicity copy. This is particularly true of architects; product, package, or trademark designers; and investors and scientists. If you find that your company employed an unusual service, seek out the people involved and interview them. Remind them, if they need reminding, that their participation also means publicity for them as well the company.

Make a Note of Those Who Express Themselves Well

During your interviews and your tours of the company, keep an ear and eye open for those who express themselves well, who have interesting stories to tell, who know the company backward and forward, anyone from the top executives to the old-timer who has been on-line for decades. Indeed, some of the most interesting interviews I have set up have been with people from the factory and workshops.

Comb the Company Files For Interesting Photographs

While going through the old records, look for historically interesting pictures taken when the company was first started, pictures of the founder, shots of the first building, the first or early assembly line, the founding employees, the first package or trademark, that sort of thing. Look for anything that might make an interesting visual story.

You also might ask retirees or those who have been with the company for many years, even those younger employees who happen to be the latest of several generations to work for the company, to bring in any old photographs they have at home. These can be publicity gems.

Get Photographs of All Old Package or Trademark Designs

One of the most interesting publicity jobs I ever had was for a famous package and trademark designer. His company had been around a long time, and consequently, many of his clients had been around a long time as well. Just browsing through the client files was a lesson in history. It was astonishing how the media ate up feature stories that were illustrated with old photographs of packages and trademarks that our great-grandparents would have found familiar. If you can't find photographs but can find samples of the old packaging or trademark, have professional photographs taken right away. Never—and I mean never—let the original samples out of your hands.

If your company is old, if your products have been around a long time, it's likely that there has been more than one package design, more than one trademark design. Collect samples or photographs of each, along with the dates they were introduced and replaced. Build a consecutive history of trademark and package design. From the history of the company and from interviews, try to find out why the designs were changed and when. If the design company that created them is still in business, make it your business to ferret out the company. Go through their files as well, and talk with anyone who remembers the project.

Take Photographs of a Product in the Making
Take a good photographer with you on your backstage tour, and have her videotape and take still photos of anything interesting going on at the plant. Be sure to get signed photo releases from anyone who is photographed before using the pictures. This is just a precaution, but a good one.

Obtain Portrait Photos of Key Personnel
Check the files for portrait photographs of all current executive personnel and anyone else who will be participating in your publicity. If none are available, have them taken. Especially make sure there are photographs of the company president and any others who might make a splash in local or national media.

Now, Review All the Information You Have Collected
Assuming that you have kept neat and accurate records of all your research, now is the time to sit down and review everything you have collected and learned. Digest it. Discuss it with colleagues, family, or friends. Then let it settle for a few days. Don't neglect this stage. The process of reviewing is often the most important stage in the long-range plans. This is the foundation upon which all your publicity will rest.

HOW TO GET PUBLICITY IDEAS
During this period, while your mind is still fresh from the research, let your brain wander. All day long, and often all night long, too, allow your thoughts to roam. You've heard of word association. Well, begin to associate the facts you've collected with publicity possibilities. At this point it doesn't matter if the ideas are impractical. They can always be trimmed from the program later.

Don't be selfish; let others in on your fun. Enlist the thoughts of your family, your friends, and even strangers. It's astonishing how someone can become caught up in your project.

Recently, I discussed a publicity project with an acquaintance I know only casually. She came up with a good idea and when days later I ran into her again, she said, "I've got another idea for you!" It, too, was a good one. Publicity people often hold these "brainstorming" sessions as a means of launching a campaign. In fact, some of my more memorable publicity events involve spending entire evenings brainstorming publicity ideas with friends.

Once you have thoroughly familiarized yourself with the company, its products, and its services, once you have allowed your thoughts to track any and every publicity possibility, it is time to begin planning your publicity program.

KEEP YOUR PUBLICITY PROGRAM REALISTIC

A publicity program is all too often like a politician's promise. It sounds good but has little to do with what really happens. Once elected, reality takes over. Many publicity programs are imaginative, well written, logical, and very impressive—but unworkable. Nothing seems to pan out according to the program.

Why? The plan may be too complicated. It may require too many people to cover all the bases. It may be too expensive. Always remember that the publicity program is there to help you get the job done. So, keep it realistic.

KEEP YOUR PUBLICITY PLAN SIMPLE

If your program is too complicated, you will probably ignore it or discard it. Certainly it's of little use. At least at the beginning, think of your publicity program as a series of things to do.

I know an executive who keeps a large desk calendar especially for his publicity program. Each day he rewrites his goals on the calendar, and below the main issues he writes what he plans to do that very day. He claims forcing himself to reword his goal each day keeps him on track. Also, he says that when one goal is reached, it is simple and natural to change the goal and keep going.

KEEP YOUR PUBLICITY PLAN FLEXIBLE

Every publicity program should be reviewed regularly, sometimes every week, for the simple reason that your goals may suddenly change.

Even without a capricious client, a random fact of life—the economy, a competitor's move, or even a major crisis—can throw your original plan into chaos. The best publicity plans, I have discovered, are flexible enough to cope with these unpredictable events. They are also geared to take advantage of new information and opportunities, just as long as these opportunities lead to your goal.

YOUR PUBLICITY PROGRAM SHOULD BE ONE OF A KIND

Don't even try to imitate someone else's publicity program. Whether yours is a deli in Queens or a multinational corporation, you must tailor your program to fit your company's specific goals, needs, personnel, geography, products, services, and style. Whatever it is, if it is part of your business, it is unique.

Sample publicity programs take up the rest of this chapter, but I don't expect you to copy them. They are offered as thought starters and to show you how each business influences the style and content of the publicity program it adopts.

Each of the following publicity programs has been designed for a different type of company, product, or service. Each program has a different goal, and consequently, the program designed for that company reflects this difference.

PUBLICITY PROGRAM FOR THE DELI

The program for the deli owner might be a trifle more complex than the one you might need:

1. Prepare a list of newspapers in the communities bordering on the Long Island Expressway (get addresses).
2. Find out from my current trucking customers which companies have newsletters (get addresses).
3. Make a separate list of all the newspapers published in Queens, including community, foreign language, and "throwaways."
4. Plan the details of a "Fame for a Day" promotion in which everyone entering the deli is asked to fill out a sheet giving pertinent information about birthdays

and wedding anniversaries. On these dates, the customers' favorite sandwiches are named after them. A large sign announcing this is placed in the deli window, and a news release giving this information, including the name of the deli, is sent to the local media, as well as to their hometown paper and any school, religious, or organizational publications they have listed on the information sheet.

5. A special calendar should be prepared to list every honored customer of Fame for a Day.
6. When feasible, expand this promotion to include local organizations observing their own special anniversaries.
7. Be sure to include a sentence reminding readers that parking space is available.

PUBLICITY PROGRAM FOR A MAGAZINE

Next, let's look at a publicity program for a magazine called SHELTER, INC. Each month SHELTER, INC. reports the latest news on architectural design, home decor, and innovative home products to a wide readership that includes both the average home owner and professionals in the trade.

Proposal

In a recent speech, the Chairman of the Association of National Advertisers warned that media salesmen are all "fishing in the same pool for the same tired fish."

The following proposal is offered as one means of finding new pools of fish to advertise in SHELTER INC. magazine, a program supplementary to, not conflicting with, the current promotional program. Although this proposal is based on one publication, the same program would also be effective for a corporation.

Objectives

1. Open doors to new advertising leads.
2. Influence the maximum number of home product advertisers with a minimum expenditure of time and money.
3. Penetrate communication barriers isolating top-echelon decision makers.

This threefold objective can be accomplished by the following plan.

I. Pinpoint promotions: Exact greater promotional mileage from the executive travel dollar to reach a cross section of locally based advertisers.

A. Schedule key speaking engagements in destination cities, and invite potential advertisers in the area as SHELTER'S special guests.

B. Arrange television appearances when sales objectives indicate their value.

II. In-depth coverage: Focus on specific trade areas to reach designated groups of home product advertisers.

A. Slant executive by-lined articles for individual trade publications, articles that command the attention and excite the interest of influential decision-makers in the industry.

B. Schedule speaking engagements before specific trade organizations in the home products field.

Pinpoint Promotions

Pinpoint promotions are surprisingly effective when adapted to current advertising sales objectives in a specific locale. Ideally, a speech before a local businessmen's organization (i.e., the Chamber of Commerce, Lions Club, or Rotary) spearheads each sales task force invasion of a city, and appropriate television and/or radio appearances (interviews or discussion shows timed and edited for business people) are scheduled at intervals throughout the promotion period.

Depending upon the type of organization, member interests, and availability of SHELTER, INC. personnel, potential speakers include:

- Publisher
- Editor-in-chief
- Advertising director
- Managing editor
- Promotion manager
- Senior editor
- Merchandising editor

A special press packet, prepared for each major speaking engagement, includes a brief biography and photograph of the speaker, a subject title, and, as a follow-up, summary remarks from the speech.

All potential advertisers in the area are SHELTER, INC. guests on the occasion of the speech and should be notified by note or word of mouth of all television and radio appearances. Interviews can be taped to send to potential customers.

In-Depth Coverage

In-depth promotional coverage of an entire industry is the answer when the advertising department plans to concentrate on either selling a new marketing area or revitalizing an existing one. Just as SHELTER, INC. is the direct route to the home product buyers, so too is the trade publication a direct route to home products manufacturers. There is always a need in any industry for a new approach to advertising or marketing problems and a fresh slant on the industry as a whole.

SHELTER, INC. executives are in an ideal position to view each home product industry objectively. This objective viewpoint, when offered in by-lined trade articles and speeches before trade organizations, proves to industry leaders that SHELTER, INC. understands their problems and talks their language—the best possible climate for follow-up direct selling of advertising space in SHELTER, INC.

PUBLICITY PROGRAM FOR A PAPER PRODUCTS COMPANY

Innovations, a paper products company, has just redesigned and repackaged their entire line. Seeing this as a perfect opportunity to push ahead of competitors, Innovations launches a full-scale publicity program aimed at both the consumer and trade.

Proposal

Recognizing the significant styling changes in Innovations' paper products and their packaging, this publicity program is designed to create the greatest possible impact on the buying public, thus increasing the demand for Innovations paper cups and plates by name. In this, a rapidly expanding market, we hope this program helps Innovations to command the leadership in both distribution and sales throughout the country.

Although research indicates that the principal occasions for using paper cups and plates are picnics, outdoor cookouts, and parties, we intend to establish in the minds of the entertaining public that Innovations paper plates and cups are both convenient and correct for indoor, as well as outdoor, entertaining.

To reach these ambitious goals, we plan to utilize consumer and trade news media, as well as television, to the greatest possible extent and, in addition, to generate enthusiasm among the nation's most influential editors through special promotions and events.

Objectives

1. Increase sales in both the outdoor and the indoor markets.
2. Upgrade the image of Innovations paper plates and cups in direct ratio to the quality, good taste, and styling currently evident in this line of paper products.
3. Give Innovations a strong identity reflected at the point of purchase.

News Media

To obtain the greatest and best possible exposure for Innovations paper plates and cups, we plan news and feature mailings to key editors for:

- Newspapers with leading circulations
- Smaller daily and weekly newspapers
- National Syndicates (AP, NEA, King Features, etc.)
- Magazines and Sunday supplements.

The last category can be of special importance because we work directly with the most influential editors on all the national publications, creating design projects and tie-ins for which they can include or feature Innovations products in their stories and photographs.

Because Innovations paper cups and plates should find a truly receptive audience in organizations and institutions, we will pay special attention to publications reaching religious organizations, the Boy Scouts and Girl Scouts, teenagers, campers, boating enthusiasts, and others.

A four-color mat release might be used to cover the nation with Innovations party ideas for special occasions.

Press Party

Because it is of vital importance that influential editors see the exciting new Innovations paper plate and cup designs when they are together, we recommend that Innovations have a press party for about 50 of the top food, entertaining, and home furnishings editors of national media in New York.

For a timely and most appropriate party, we might have a "June in January" party on an enclosed patio or in a public place surrounded by lush vegetation. For a realistic effect, we might have records of bird songs and the humming of insects. For atmosphere, we could hang lanterns and feature the most appropriate new designs.

As a special gift to the media, we might give them a set of Innovations plates and cups and/or something related, such as a gold-plated cup dispenser, small golden eagle pins (in which case we could feature the patriotic pattern at dinner), or barbecue accessories to remind them of the special barbecue design on both the cups and plates.

An unusual product display might be achieved if instead of a rigid exhibition of the four new Innovations patterns, we hang dozens of plates and cups from the ceiling either singly or together, giving the effect of a mobile.

The press kits we distribute to the editors should include:
- In-use photographs with captions of each of the new Innovations designs.
- Stories on why these designs were selected and how they were created.
- Party ideas for carrying out the theme of each new pattern. For example, to showcase the Tuscany line, serve hero sandwiches, small bottles of Chianti, and coffee. The party room should be decorated as a romantic Italian restaurant, and the background music should be appropriately Italian.

Follow-up Promotion

Four major mailings, one on each of the new designs, are scheduled at intervals of about every two months and are directed to distinctly different media lists. These mailings include photographs of party preparations featuring an Innovations pattern with a detailed description of how to achieve the resulting effect.

In May, a barbecue featuring the paper plates and cups designed for a barbecue is a natural for a teenage party in the backyard or on the beach. A special party favor is a sun visor personalized with the stenciled name of the guest.

In July, for the children, a Zoo party is exciting, especially if each guest receives an animal mask and animal "ears" and "tail" to wear. To carry out the theme of this party, the Zoo pattern is most appropriate.

In September, a sidewalk cafe patio party is a perfect setting for a photograph featuring the Paris Bistro design.

In November, for a more formal note, the Federal-style patterned plates and cups add a note of sophistication at an indoor party. Small bronze eagles decorate the tables along with Federal-style candle holders.

Television

To obtain the greatest possible publicity mileage from the executive travel dollar, we arrange for representatives of Innovation products to appear on television in key market cities to discuss the current trend of informality in formal entertaining or other subjects related to Innovations products and their use in and outside the home.

To maintain continuity of television promotion for Innovations throughout the country, we provide television personalities with a script written about the multiple uses of Innovations products. In addition, we send them an attractive and interesting prop related to the product that can be displayed on television.

We look into the feasibility of mailings to giveaway and children's shows, and if the resultant publicity warrants, we supply the producer with enough product for an after-show party.

Tie-ins

As we get into this publicity program, there are numerous possibilities for tie-in publicity features. The most appropriate tie-in, perhaps, is with food products, such as fruits or soups. It is very possible that we can get a tie-in with one of New York's leading Fifth Avenue women's specialty stores.

The Trade

The trade press is an important avenue of publicity in the promotion of Innovations paper plates and cups because it is through these publications that we can show directly how

Innovations new surface designs and package designs can increase sales at the point of purchase and how Innovations displays can be used most effectively for tie-in sales.

General announcement releases, as well as exclusive stories, are written for all related trade papers, including:

▬ Grocery, department, and variety stores
▬ Packaging and design
▬ Sales promotion, advertising, and merchandising
▬ Housewares

Some of the press releases are:

▬ Announcement of the new product designs, package designs, and display units for point-of-purchase promotions
▬ Description and promotional value of the POP visuals
▬ Photographs of vertical shelf displays
▬ Case histories

PROGRAM FOR A VINYL-COATED WALL-COVERING COMPANY

Springtex, a wall-coverings company, would like to open new markets and create a higher profile with consumers, decorators, and distributors.

Objectives

I. Upgrade all Springtex wall coverings for greater designer acceptance.

A. Press introductions for all new products and/or designs

B. Special tie-ins with prestige designer organizations and home furnishings events

C. Feature stories tailored to quality home publications

II. Open new markets and solidify present markets.

A. Speaking engagements before business organizations arranged for company executives during prescheduled business trips

B. Dealer promotion kits to include display, promotion, and merchandising ideas and suggested advertising copy for television, radio, and newspapers

C. Stories and articles aimed at specific trade publications

III. Increase consumer demand.

    A. Feature stories and photographs provided in a continuing flow to newspapers, magazines, wire services, television, and radio

    B. Television and radio appearances arranged for designated company executives during prescheduled business trips

IV. Increase corporate prestige in the business and financial world.

    A. Releases sent to business and financial editors on all corporate news of a prestige-building nature

    B. Statements by specified Springtex executives designed to make them the spokespeople for the industry

    C. Exclusive executive by-lined articles written for specific business publications.

Feature Story and Picture Ideas

■ Give Your Kitchen an Artist's Touch: Using easel and stretched canvas as props, show step-by-step process of how this wall-covering product is designed.

■ It's What's Inside That Counts: Show versatility of product as a liner for drawers and shelves.

■ A Real Cool Idea: A "how-to" story on making window shades and draw roofs for patios that keep out heat by reflecting the sun's rays.

■ A Colorful Wrap-up: Demonstrate how squares of wall covering can be used as brightly colored wrappings for packages.

■ Make It Rich: Picture story on the best methods for covering inexpensive and/or unpainted furniture with Springtex for professional results.

■ A Shade of Difference: Give a room the decorator touch by covering a window shade with Springtex.

■ Here's One for the Books: Cover cardboard file boxes with Springtex to give the appearance of a matched set of books.

■ All in a Day's Work: Cover file cabinets, desks, tables, and matching desk accessories for office or home.

■ There's No Ceiling on Beauty: Take demonstration photographs to show how simple it is to cover a ceiling with prepasted Springtex wall coverings.

■ A Change in the Weather . . . A Change in the Scene: Show how, with a switch to a seasonal wallpaper even on one wall and the rotating of accessories, the entire mood of a room can be changed with ease.

Panel a Room with Paper: Show how wood-grained wallpaper can give a drab room the richness of a paneled library.

MERCHANDISING AND PROMOTIONAL IDEAS (PUBLICITY STORIES ON EACH)

1. Introduce new Artist Original designs.
2. Create an aura of glamor and quality by presenting new designs as examples of fine art.
3. Frame designs for window and in-store displays.
4. Design hangtags and counter cards as artist's palettes.
5. Gifts for dealers and/or media: Select the brightest and most seasonal patterns to be used for wrapping Christmas or birthday gifts.
6. Design Springtex-covered press kits that can be reused by the recipient as telephone book covers.

PUBLICITY PROGRAM FOR A RESTAURANT

The owners of Cafe Elegant faced strong competition from many new and very trendy restaurants. They decided to launch a publicity program that would project an image of Cafe Elegant as a fashionable, even exclusive, dining spot and a favorite of celebrities.

Objectives

I. Newspapers
   A. Large dailies
   B. Neighborhood and suburban
II. Television and radio

METRO PAPERS (LARGE DAILY NEWSPAPERS)

1. Send exclusive column notes on meetings and activities being conducted in the restaurant to each columnist regularly or whenever such occasions occur.
2. Send general news stories to each newspaper (city editor) on special news events.
   a. Club meetings held in the restaurant
   b. Special promotions, such as contests

    c. Special interviews with celebrities

    d. Special stories about plans for holidays

3. Send picture (8 × 10 black and white glossies) to picture editors (exclusive to each editor).

    a. News events or meetings (speakers, etc.)

    b. People of news value—candid shots

    c. Humorous or unusual photographs of events

    d. Special-day pictures: holiday, birthday, anniversary

4. Send special feature stories to feature writers on individual newspapers.

    a. Women's page editors

        (1) Society notes and pictures

        (2) Interviews with newsworthy women

        (3) Human interest interviews with women employees

        (4) Cooking tips from chef

        (5) Club meetings held at restaurant

    b. Sports editors

        (1) Sports column notes emanating from restaurant

        (2) Reports on sports meetings

        (3) Interviews with sports personalities

    c. Fashion editors

        (1) Report on fashion shows

        (2) Social report—"Who's wearing what"

    d. Nightclub and restaurant editors

        (1) General stories on entertainment

        (2) Stories on new policies

        (3) Exclusive feature stories on business

        (4) Column notes on nightlife

NEIGHBORHOOD AND SUBURBAN NEWSPAPERS

1. Send exclusive column notes to columnists on people and events in their coverage area.

2. Send general news stories to each newspaper about people in their coverage area, people who visit your restaurant.

3. Send neighborhood and suburban newspapers all the news of people and events of interest to readers in their news coverage area.

LOCAL TELEVISION AND RADIO STATIONS

1. Contact shows for interviews or participation.
   a. Women's shows
   b. Club shows
   c. Disk jockey shows
   d. Sports shows
   e. Giveaway shows
   f. Game shows
   g. Variety and talk shows
   h. News shows
2. Send news items.
   a. News editors
   b. Club editors
   c. Women's editors
   d. Sports editors
3. Publicize special events.
   a. Cooking demonstrations
   b. Professional advice: How to plan a luncheon

NATIONAL TELEVISION AND RADIO NETWORKS

Plan the same campaign as for local stations whenever the news item or interview is of sufficient national interest.

CHAPTER PERSPECTIVE

This chapter took the goals you formed in the previous chapter and showed you how to build a unique and workable publicity plan for your company, product, or service. This is the plan that will guide you in all your daily decisions throughout your publicity campaign. In addition, the information you collected to plan your publicity will give an extra dimension and add interest to your contacts with the media and to the preparation of query letters, stories, and fact sheets for the media.

Meet John Diggs

INTRODUCTION AND MAIN POINTS

In this chapter you will meet someone like yourself who is learning the fundamentals of getting publicity for his company and product. John Diggs and his company are fictitious, of course, but the product has been around in one form or another for hundreds of years: the shovel.

Before you say, "Good grief! Why a shovel?" I must tell you that I selected this particular product for the very reason that it has been around such a long time. I hope that by seeing how John Diggs promotes the shovel, you will realize that regardless of how old and ordinary a product, there are always methods for getting publicity for it.

After studying the material in this chapter:

▬ You will see what alerted John Diggs to the need for publicity.

▬ You will see how John Diggs pinpoints his sales problems and sets his goals.

▬ You will see how John Diggs collects background information and photographs for publicity stories and fact sheets.

▬ You will learn what stories John Diggs writes in advance of his actual publicity campaign.

▬ You will learn how John Diggs uses brainstorming sessions to come up with publicity ideas.

▬ You will learn how John Diggs plans his publicity program.

John Diggs has been in the shovel-manufacturing business for a long time. He is president of one of the oldest and most firmly established companies of its kind, which was handed down to him by his father and grandfather. His company, the Diggs Shovel Company, Inc., makes a good, sturdy, tempered-steel shovel with a strong wooden handle.

The Diggs Shovel Company has had the same customers—industrial, agricultural, and retail—for many, many years. These customers have long been reliable and regular in their orders. So much so that Diggs Shovel Company executives have become complacent. They have taken too much for granted.

Now, suddenly, sales have slipped. The last time John Diggs looked at his sales chart, it was frowning.

The competition has become greater and greater. Electric shovels, snow throwers, and even plastic shovels have made serious inroads both on his old customers and on the number of new customers being brought into the company.

Accustomed over the years to a certain pattern of selling and promotion, good, old, standard promotions that served the company well during his father's and grandfather's time, John Diggs has not taken any particular measures to offset his competitors' gains.

Now the situation is critical. John Diggs must do something—fast.

Of course, he plans to advertise but he believes this is not enough. He wants publicity, but his resources of time and labor are limited. Therefore, he plans to target his publicity to make every story, every bit of free publicity count for something.

First, he must define his objectives so the people in his company—and he, himself—work toward the same goal.

JOHN DIGGS PINPOINTS HIS SALES PROBLEMS

Asking himself why sales are slipping and studying his sales and marketing situation with his team of executives, John Diggs analyzes his primary sales problems and examines possible solutions. As a means of solidifying his thoughts, Diggs writes a memorandum to himself, which he may or may not later distribute to his top executives. You may also find writing your ideas down on paper helpful.

Memorandum To Myself and Executive Officers

1. IMPROVE OUR PRODUCT AND COMPANY IMAGE

The Diggs Shovel Company has the reputation (earned, I admit) for being out of step with the times. Instead of fighting this "old-fashioned" image, we now plan to capitalize upon it.

We will promote the idea that old-fashioned is better, that old-fashioned means "back to basics" or the natural way of doing things. We will stress the idea that the original hand-driven shovel, especially one as well constructed and reliable as the Diggs shovel, is an important part of the current back to basics trend to physical fitness and energy conservation.

Because of improper use and handling, the shovel has an undeserved reputation for creating back strain and other physical problems. We plan to educate the current and potential shovel user in the product's proper use and care and, indeed, to promote methods of using the shovel to improve one's health and create general physical well-being.

2. OPEN NEW MARKET SEGMENTS

There are many new companies out there in the various shovel-using markets, including government agencies, that have never heard of the Diggs Shovel Company. We plan to remedy this by getting publicity for the Diggs Company and its superior shovel in all media that reach these markets. We intend to inform these potential customers about the Diggs shovel in every way possible, first by making them familiar with the name of the company and then telling them of its long-standing reputation as a reliable supplier.

The objectives are to overcome the technological gap created by power tools; to offset sales of plastic snow shovels; to get users back to the hand-driven shovel; and to prove that the Diggs shovel costs less to buy and less to operate and is more durable and reliable than other choices. We also intend to stress the health and safety aspects of the do-it-yourself shovel.

We intend to get as much publicity in the general consumer media as possible to attract queries and orders from new market segments we have not as yet identified. We will then devise publicity and special projects specifically aimed at capitalizing on these special-interest market segments.

To get more from our advertising dollar, we propose to obtain consumer and trade publicity for our advertising and sales promotion campaigns to make them even more far-reaching and cost effective.

3. PRESELL DECISION MAKERS

A number of new personnel have moved into the job slots formerly held by faithful Diggs business contacts and they know little or nothing about the Diggs shovel. As a result, sales personnel take too much time selling the Diggs shovel, competing with newer features and names and more aggressive advertising, sales, and promotional programs. Some old contacts are still in buying positions but no longer make the buying decisions, and our sales reps are hesitant to go over their heads to the truly influential personnel for fear of damaging their current relationships.

To reach new decision makers and to tell our sales message even behind the closed doors of the higher echelon of decision makers in industry and agribusiness, we propose to create news of interest about the Diggs Shovel Company and to report it to these decision makers through trade publications edited for and aimed at their specific needs and interests.

To remedy those situations in which the salesperson can reach the decision maker but finds too much time is spent in selling the product, we will help presell the product by adding necessary facts and selling information to every trade press release sent out.

When the elusive decision maker is the buyer for a retail store or retail chain of stores, we plan to ensure that retail stores stock the Diggs shovel by pressuring store buyers through the next level of decision makers: their customers. We propose to do this by preselling the trendsetters and opinion makers within the consumer public. To do this we will devise special projects to elicit interest and excitement among trendsetters to reach and presell the decision makers in the families.

ADVANCE PREPARATIONS

Your publicity plan itself is very important, but the gathering of facts and the analysis of how these facts can be adapted to company and product publicity are often the most useful part of your program. During your advance preparations, you rivet the attention of employees and draw them into a concentrated companywide publicity effort. Consequently, you should take your advance preparations very seriously. John Diggs does, as you can see from the following.

SCOUR THE COMPANY FOR NEWS

Scour the company for news. This news might be about people, anniversaries, new service offers, new merchandising offers, or new personnel—anything that instills in decision makers the idea of product superiority, people superiority, service superiority, source superiority, or price superiority so that our publicity can begin as quickly as possible, remembering that each news story should carry a hidden sales message based on one or more of our sales needs and requirements.

▬ Every department head must search for possible news stories after you alert them about what they should look for as potential news.

▬ Every department head must think about possible publicity stories that they might report and/or create for the business press, consumer press, or television and radio.

▬ The advertising, merchandising, and promotion departments must think of new ways we might offer services to the customer that could be reported as news.

PREPARE BIOGRAPHIES OF ALL PARTICIPATING PERSONNEL

▬ Prepare personal biographies on myself, John Diggs, the owner, and every member of the executive staff who might ultimately represent this company in press interviews and television and radio interviews. This includes men and women throughout the company who have been with the organization for many years or whose families have worked for the company for more than one generation.

▬ Also, prepare a biography of my grandfather, the founder of the Diggs Shovel Company, and my father, who succeeded him as president of the company.

▬ Prepare a fact sheet to accompany each biography, providing a quick reference to dates, places, and happenings.

PREPARE A HISTORY OF THE COMPANY

▬ Prepare a history of the Diggs company going back to the founder, and look for and highlight interesting facts about the origin of the company. Be especially alert for any anniversaries such as the anniversary of the company, of the first shovel manufactured, or of the first shovel sold.

▬ Prepare a fact sheet for quick reference.

PREPARE A HISTORY OF THE SHOVEL

▬ Prepare a history of the shovel, "digging" back into ancient times to ferret out interesting anecdotes about the shovel and its use, perhaps by interesting persons. Perhaps someone has written about the shovel or mentioned it in historical writings.

▬ Prepare a fact sheet on the history of the shovel.

PLAN TELEVISION AND RADIO INTERVIEW POSSIBILITIES

▬ Consider every individual in the company as a possible effective interviewee for television and radio. Judge their effectiveness by title (the authority they have to speak for the company), by their presence and how they express themselves, and by their experience with the company and the interesting stories they tell.

▬ Plan visuals (photographs, samples, and demonstrations) that make the interviews even more interesting.

▬ Write sample letters to television and radio interviewers suggesting interviews with members of our company.

WRITE COLUMN NOTES AND FEATURE MATERIAL

▬ Check all biographical and historical material gathered for any interesting anecdotes that might make good media "fillers" and column notes.

▬ Look for interesting and/or unusual anecdotes during any and all future research that might make good filler copy for editors or interesting tidbits for interviews.

▬ Prepare feature story ideas and feature stories that would be appropriate "exclusives" for special-interest media.

SEARCH FILES FOR HISTORICAL PHOTOGRAPHS

▬ Check all files, even family records, for photographs taken of the company personnel and buildings during the years of its origin and growth.

▬ Take professional-quality photographs of the Diggs shovel, preferably being used in unusual ways, for unexpected reasons, and by interesting and attractive people.

▬ Have photographs taken of the Diggs shovel to emphasize in both trade and feature pictures the advantages of the shovel.

PREPARE INTERESTING CASE HISTORIES
▬ Get the sales department to search their records and speak with old customers to see if they are still using Diggs shovels bought many years ago.

▬ Find individuals, organizations, and companies that use the Diggs shovels in interesting ways or for unusual purposes.

▬ Look for production facts and figures on the costs to buy and operate the Diggs' shovel versus any other shovel equipment on the market.

GET PUBLICITY FOR OUR ADVERTISING AND MERCHANDISING PROGRAMS
▬ The advertising department should report in-depth about any new plans for an advertising campaign.

▬ Get photos and facts on any new merchandising materials available to customers. Alert departmental principals to report all future merchandising plans.

CHECK FOR RECORDS SET
▬ Get facts and figures together to see if we recently have achieved any sort of record in sales or production.

▬ Check to see how many shovels have been manufactured and/or sold by the Diggs Shovel Company. This might provide us with an interesting news announcement. If not, have that department, as well as other departments, remain alert for any sort of record of possible interest to the media.

PLAN THE APPROPRIATE RELEASE OF POSITIVE FINANCIAL NEWS
Although ours is a privately owned company and therefore under no legal obligation to report our financial news, we should consider reporting any news that makes our company look financially strong and reliable. This is important because most people want to buy from a company they know will be around for a long time.

LOCATE OUTSIDE PERSONNEL TO HELP WITH PROMOTION
▬ Consider and start to look for outside personnel or experts we may need.

▬ Locate a health or physical fitness expert or a sports physician who is available to go on television to illustrate the proper way to use a shovel.

CHECK TRAVEL SCHEDULES OF ALL DIGGS EXECUTIVES

Check the travel schedules of all Diggs executives who are available for television, radio, and press interviews during their visits to customer communities.

PLAN BRAINSTORMING SESSIONS FOR PUBLICITY IDEAS

▪Begin a dialogue with employees, family, and friends. Get everyone in on the act because some of the most interesting ideas come from the most unexpected people. Encourage ideas from those of varying ages and interests so that our publicity reflects the greatest possible variety of ages, experience, and interests.

▪Get family, friends, and employees from research and production, as well as front office departments, to think of new ways the shovel might be used, ideas that might be used to promote it, and possible changes to the shovel that might, without altering production significantly, make the shovel more interesting to potential buyers.

▪Get the sales, advertising, merchandising, and promotion departments to begin thinking of new services that might be offered customers and potential customers, services that can be reported as news in the business press.

▪Ask for ideas that reflect the unique qualities of the Diggs shovel (safety, flexibility, cost, and use) and ideas that might be built around new services that any department in the company might offer to influence potential customers.

PREPARE PRESS KITS

Prepare press kits for everyone who will appear before the media—newspapers, trade publications, television, and radio—for them to keep with them at all times should an opportunity for free publicity come up at a moment's notice. This should include much of the information and visuals that have been gathered during the advance preparations. This maximizes our travel dollar.

These press kits should contain copies of each of the previously mentioned histories, biographies, fact sheets, press releases, photographs, and column notes, as well as anything else that might be of interest to the media.

PREPARE PUBLICITY MAILING LISTS

1. Wire services
2. News syndicates
3. Weekly and suburban newspapers
4. Selected daily papers
5. Consumer publications
6. Trade publications
7. Television and radio (national and local)
8. Publications interested in the personal activities of company executives and other employees directly involved with the company

PREPARE FOR MAILINGS

Get labels or envelopes ready so that a mailing can be sent out at a moment's notice, or contact a mailing company for a plan and work it out in detail.

PUBLICITY PROGRAM FOR THE JOHN DIGGS SHOVEL COMPANY

Objectives

- Update and improve the company and product image.
- Open new market segments.
- Presell decision makers.
- Educate our customers in the proper use of the shovel.
- Promote our advertising, and give it extra mileage.

Proposal

To cut our publicity to a size we can handle while reaching all our goals, we will introduce a new theme promotion: Back to Basics.

Back to Basics

Because the shovel has been around for such a long time, we propose to use this Back to Basics theme in all our promotions, special events, and projects and as our sales message theme in all our news and feature stories.

The idea behind this Back to Basics theme is that returning to the hand-driven shovel cuts costs, saves on electricity, and at the same time promotes good health and physical well-being.

We propose that our Back to Basics theme be applied in several different ways:

■ Conserve energy: Because it is hand operated and muscle driven, there is no cost for fuel or electrical energy.

■ Protect the environment: By using the Diggs shovel, you are not using fuel; therefore, you contribute to the protection of the environment.

■ Improve personal health and physical well-being: Instead of relying on machines to do your work, the Diggs shovel gives you the opportunity to set up your personal "health club" in your own backyard.

The Back to Basics theme also gives us the opportunity to stress the durability, flexibility, and low initial and operating costs of the basic shovel.

To get this Back to Basics theme across to all our market segments, we propose publicity in related trade publications, newspapers, consumer magazines, television, and radio.

We propose to report all news naturally generated throughout the company, inserting the Back to Basics message in everything released to the media and creating news through special projects, promotions, and events with a news factor built into them, a news factor stressing the Back to Basics theme.

We propose to begin thinking publicity immediately and to begin right now to get the entire company and its personnel thinking of ways and means of getting publicity.

We propose that our first press release be sent out no later than October 15.

John Diggs' Publicity Plan

REPORT ALL COMPANY NEWS

Write news releases on all news naturally generated by the company, and send these releases at appropriate intervals to the appropriate trade media and consumer media.

■ Announcement of all new and promoted personnel
■ New construction
■ Moving
■ Research and development projects

ANNOUNCE DIGGS' NEW BACK TO BASICS PROMOTIONAL THEME

1. Local newspapers
2. Local television and radio news editors
3. Wire services
4. Large metropolitan daily newspapers
5. National syndicates
6. Trade publications: industrial and agricultural
7. Special-interest publications
   a. Environment
   b. Conservation
   c. Physical fitness
   d. Health

PLAN SPECIAL PROJECTS TO PROMOTE THE BACK TO BASICS THEME

Organize a special emergency shovel crew to clean the sidewalks of senior citizens.

SET UP BACK TO BASICS TELEVISION AND RADIO INTERVIEWS

Send query letters or call program directors and/or interview show contacts on television and radio stations, and set up interviews for company personnel visiting these cities. Pay particular attention to cities where decision makers are located, and notify them of the interviews.

1. Local television and radio interviews should be set up first to provide on-air experience.
2. Contact regional and national television shows.
3. List possible interview topics:
   a. Demonstrating the proper use of a shovel
   b. Choosing a strong-handled shovel
   c. Showing a videotape of the Back to Basics emergency shovel corps in action: shoveling sidewalks for snowbound senior citizens and from anywhere the public reports that snow needs to be removed to cut down on accidents. (There could be a snow "hotline" for Back to Basic emergency teams.)

PLAN REGULARLY SCHEDULED BACK TO BASICS PRESS RELEASES

These could be weekly, monthly, or bimonthly, but they should be good, solid news announcements or feature stories, not just releases to fill a void.

RELEASE ALL BACK TO BASICS NEWS STORIES AS THEY COME UP

1. Announce interviews.
2. Report newsworthy statements made during interviews.
3. Report speeches made by Diggs people in press releases.
4. Report all emergency corps activities.
5. Announce related activities.

INTEREST EDITORS IN FEATURE STORIES ON BACK TO BASICS

1. Interview a physical fitness expert on shoveling as a good outdoor exercise for keeping fit.
2. Interview a sports physician on the proper use of a shovel.
3. Interview a well-known environmentalist on how hand-operated shovels help keep the environment safe.
4. During a gasoline shortage, have conservationists explain how using hand-driven tools can help conserve energy.
5. During summer brownouts, set up an interview with a representative of the local power company to explain how hand-driven tools cut down on electricity use during shortages.

TELEVISION AND RADIO

Set up television and radio interview shows for the company president and any other executives connected with the company and product.

NEWSPAPERS AND MAGAZINES

Contact editors of shelter and family publications and other consumer magazines offering "exclusive" stories and pictures. We do this several months in advance of the release date.

NEWS RELEASES

Mail or deliver news releases so they are on the editors' desks in plenty of time to meet their own specific deadlines.

CHAPTER PERSPECTIVE

This chapter took a fictitious executive, John Diggs, over the same hurdles you will face in planning and preparing for your publicity. In the following chapters, you will see how John Diggs interprets the advice and uses the information provided to publicize his own product, the shovel.

Getting Started

INTRODUCTION AND MAIN POINTS

In this chapter we deal with the mechanics of setting up shop. This involves not only getting your office space functioning smoothly, but organizing your available human resources so that you can get the maximum return on your investment.

After studying the material in this chapter:

■ You will be able to set up your office space so that your press releases can be written and processed as quickly as possible.

■ You will be able to set up a communications system so that you can instantly be in touch with the media in order to take advantage of every publicity opportunity.

■ You will be able to set up a support system of outside services that will back you up whenever and however they are needed.

■ You will be able to organize your available human resources so that everyone involved is able to produce at his or her maximum capacity.

A successful press agent I once knew was proud that he operated "out of his hat." Night after night he could be seen in chic restaurants and nightclubs, a telephone always nearby. This was fine for him because his specialty was column notes about personalities and nightlife. He could simply call them in to the columnists. Anyone serious about getting business publicity needs a place to hang his hat, however.

Why is it so important to have a publicity "office"? Assuming you have collected all the information you need to start your publicity, I'd like to ask you this question: where is it?

Let me guess. If you're working at home, the first material you gathered is neatly filed along with documents related to your home. Some of it is probably in the stack of material waiting to be filed. The tapes you haven't gotten around to transcribing are in your bureau under your socks. There may be information with the mail on the hall table.

If you work out of a business office, the information you collected is probably distributed between the files in your office and your home, your desk drawers, and perhaps in the offices and files of anyone who has helped you. Actually, you're probably not quite sure where anything is.

Are you set up to begin your business publicity? What do you think?

PUBLICITY NEEDS A PLACE TO CALL HOME

If you have collected all the information important to publicity for your company, personnel, product, and services, you need to keep it someplace where you can get to it quickly and easily. It won't do you or your publicity efforts one iota of good if it has been misplaced or if it has disappeared into someone else's files. Whether you are working alone or with a staff, you need a central location where all publicity research and information can be stored and retrieved at will.

Whether your publicity space is a corner of your bedroom, the back of your store, or an office within a company, you need to plan it in advance and to acquire the equipment necessary to run your publicity efficiently, and you need office supplies where you can get to them fast.

A CHECKLIST OF OFFICE ESSENTIALS

"Be prepared" has not become one of the world's most famous slogans for nothing. When the need for publicity arises, you want to be able to concentrate on the goal, not on getting settled and organizing supplies. Trying to play catch-up in this business is foolish and costly. Don't make this mistake.

You Need a Central Source for All Your Research

A filing cabinet comes to mind, a filing cabinet that belongs to publicity and to publicity alone. Collect all the facts and information you have rounded up to date, and organize it so that, when the need arises, you can find it. If you don't have a filing cabinet, use a sturdy box: anything is better than having everything strewn all over the place. You may find you need a file for 3 × 5 cards. Since I carry these with me all the time for taking notes, my small file cabinet is indispensable.

You Need a Surface on Which to Write

Ideally this surface is a desk, a strong desk with a nice, large work surface. If you set up an office at home, even an old table will do, but not the one in the dining room. You need a desk that doesn't have to be cleared several times a day. If you have to buy a desk, be sure it fits both the space you have and the space you need. You can easily make a desk using a flush door purchased at a local lumberyard, supported at each end by two, two-drawer filing cabinets. This way you can solve two problems at once.

You Will Find a Personal Computer To Be Indispensable

If you already have a PC—great; and if you know how to use all its functions, you're *really* in business. If you don't have a PC, seriously consider purchasing one. Today, personal computers can be found in most offices. In a very few years, no business—large or small—will be able to function without one.

With your PC, you will be able to "file" your notes for instant retrieval. You will be able to keep your mailing lists up to date and print mailing labels with a few keystrokes. Also, you will be able to select specific editors to receive specific stories. This would be enough for many of us, but there are myriad other exciting and work-saving PC programs already available—with many more on the way.

For example, it won't be long before you'll be given access through your PC and your telephone modem to "libraries without walls" which already are beginning to appear in schools and businesses. Soon these high-technology centers will be available to personal computers everywhere.

Imaging, the general term for making electronic copies of physical documents by presenting them to a scanner, will soon be widely available. Imaging will make the input, display, and transmission of documents and illustrations available to anyone with a PC. Library resources will become available far beyond the library's immediate geographic area, and your branch offices will be able to gain access to printed information regardless of where it is physically stored.

Once your business begins to grow, you might consider subscribing to a data bank—an information retrieval service that serves up articles published in magazines and newspapers. And with a printer, you can print out the transmitted information into hard copy.

With a personal computer and a modem you will also be able to communicate with editors and collaborate on promotional tie-ins with other publicity and public relations people throughout the country. Link into an "electronic bulletin board," "computer conference," or "electronic mail exchange," and you can connect with people of like interests and goals thousands of miles away. Several networks—both national and international—are already available to PC owners. But be wary. Add telephone charges to the cost of a subscription to a network, and the total can be rather steep. When you feel it's worth the money to subscribe to a computer network, be sure to do your homework. Networks vary greatly as to services and costs. Be sure to subscribe to the one that is absolutely right for you. When you are ready to take the plunge, you will find that networks advertise in computer magazines—sometimes even in newspapers. Get information on all of them.

Whether or not you are ready to subscribe to a bulletin board or a data bank, seriously consider what a computer can do to speed up your day-to-day output of correspondence and releases. Once you own a word processing program, you'll wonder how you ever got along without it. With the "cut and paste" feature, which allows you to make copy changes and corrections easily, writing and printing become a snap.

A "mail merge" program allows you to personalize all kinds of business form letters, giving a small business the large business touch. If you opt for the mailing label function, you can produce as many labels as you want, of any size or shape. And you can print a message on the bottom of each mailing label, such as "Urgent—Open Immediately."

Communication Is the Core of Publicity

Publicity is a business of communications. A private-line telephone is indispensable, and it should sit on or near your desk so you can readily take notes. You probably need an answering machine or answering service as well. When a reporter or editor wants to reach you, it's wise to be available.

The FAX is another invaluable communication device. All you need is a FAX machine and the FAX telephone number of the person to whom you wish to send a message. If you are not ready to invest in a machine, many neighborhood stores are now equipped to FAX your letters and releases for a fee.

Press Releases Need To Be Typed

The editor won't see your typewriter or word processor, but she will see the way it prints. If you buy a word processor, stay away from dot matrix printers. Editors don't like dot matrix, and some won't even accept it. If you use a typewriter, use plain pica type, never fancy or unusual type. Editors also want clean, black-on-white copy.

You Need Office Supplies

Many beginning publicists fail to realize that they need all the basic office supplies and equipment that any other full-fledged office requires. When you promise an editor a biography, a news release, or a feature story, this doesn't mean next week. It means today or, at the very least, tomorrow. You won't have time to run down to the stationery store for white copy paper. You want it where you can get to it, fast.

BOND PAPER

Get at least a ream (large package) of 16- to 20-pound white bond paper, $8\frac{1}{2} \times 11$ inches size, for the final draft of your news release, feature story, or picture caption, the copy the editor receives. Never use erasable bond, colored, or onion-skin paper for your press releases.

INEXPENSIVE COPY PAPER

You'll probably use a lot of copy paper before you come up with a suitable final draft of each press release; so use paper that is as cheap as possible. In fact, for this purpose you can use anything you have around the house, or anyone else's house, for that matter. When you run out of inexpensive copy paper or scrap paper, you might buy some manila second sheets. This is newspaper-grade stock and inexpensive. You can use this for file copies as well. Even if you use a word processor and therefore don't need copy paper to write and edit your copy, it's a good idea to run off a reference and backup copy for your files.

ENVELOPES

You need two types of envelopes: number 10 (long white) envelopes for mailing your press releases and 9 × 12 brown envelopes for mailing photographs. You might also consider buying first-class, prestamped number 10 envelopes from the post office. You may be able to have your name and address preprinted on them.

BUSINESS STATIONERY

Eventually you will want some business stationery imprinted with your company name, address, and telephone number. You will also want a matching number 10 envelope imprinted with your return address.

POSTAGE

You know you're going to be sending out mail and whether it will be a few single letters or press releases or a large mailing. You can cut down on a last-minute rush by buying sufficient first-class postage well in advance. As your publicity gets underway, you might find it expedient to rent a postage meter. If you want more information on postage meters and where you can rent one, write to: Pitney Bowes, Walnut and Pacific Sts., Stamford, CT 06904. Also, you can cut down on wasted postage or having letters returned for insufficient postage simply by buying and using an accurate postal scale.

REFERENCE BOOKS

You will need a good dictionary, telephone books, and a secretarial or writer's handbook to guide you in such writer's rules as punctuation and capitalization. If you want to save yourself trips to the library, you may want to invest in the media directories you will use most often. These are often expensive, so be very careful in your choice. Remember that some directories specialize in the print media while others concentrate on television and radio. Do some serious research at your local library before you decide. Also, remember that your lists must continually be updated.

APPOINTMENT BOOK OR DESK CALENDAR
This is imperative because you need as much help as you can get to keep your schedule manageable.

RUBBER STAMPS
You need a rubber stamp made up with your name, address, and telephone number, as well as DO NOT BEND and FIRST CLASS MAIL stamps, and a black ink pad.

MISCELLANEOUS
You need rubber cement to attach picture captions to photographs. Don't forget the essentials: carbon paper, writing pads for taking notes, mailing labels, 3 × 5 cards, pens, pencils, paper clips, stapler and staples, and so on. If you have a typewriter, you need ribbons, preferably carbon ribbons, and if you have a word processor, you need diskettes and ribbons for your printer.

Every Publicity Enterprise Needs a Support System
Even the largest public relations office subcontracts some of the publicity tasks that require a certain expertise, equipment, or training. Before you go any further, make sure you know where you can get this professional assistance and how much it costs. You may not need these services right away, but you should be able to reach the best for your purposes at a moment's notice and know, in advance, how much it costs.

SECRETARIAL SERVICE
You, your family, or your staff may be able to handle all the typing and filing that needs to be done, but just in case your publicity schedule is overloaded and you need a backup, it's a good idea to find out in advance the secretarial services available in your community, the types of services they offer, and the rates they charge. If you hire a part-time typist who works at home, make sure the word processor or typewriter, as well as the typist's skills, meets your requirements.

OFFSET PRINTING
The number of copies of the press release you plan to send out determines the type of service you require for making multiple copies. If only a few copies are required or if you are sending "exclusive" stories, then leave this to the typist or

photocopy machine. However, if you need large quantities for a mass mailing, look into the prices, quality, availability, and speed of offset printing. Be sure the copies are as close to the original typing as possible: good contrast of black on white.

PHOTOCOPY CENTERS
A professional photographer provides the photographs agreed upon, but if you want enough copies of pictures for a mass mailing, you certainly want to check into the nearest photocopy centers. Check out the break-even point at which it pays you to switch from individually printed pictures to large quantities of glossy prints. Be sure to check out the quality of the photographs before you make your final decision. You can find the names of photocopy centers in your local Yellow Pages. For more information on what to look for and what to expect, read Chapter VIII on photographs.

PROFESSIONAL PHOTOGRAPHERS
You never know when you will need a professional photographer or what sort of expertise will be required. For instance, a news photographer can handle most publicity shots, but if you want professional-quality photographs of your product, you want a photographer who specializes in this.

MAILING SERVICES
If you are a small, local business you may never need a mailing service, but don't count on it. You might just come up with a bright idea for regional publicity and find yourself unable to execute it simply because you don't have the human resources necessary to get out a mailing. What a shame that would be, and it takes so little time to get a mailing service lined up in advance.

PRESS CLIPPING BUREAUS
Just in case you don't know what a press clipping bureau does, it checks thousands of daily and weekly newspapers, trade, professional, and technical publications, consumer magazines—even network news and talk shows—for mentions of any company that retains the service. If you hire a press clipping bureau, you tell them precisely what to look for and, if you are wise, even send them copies of any publicity

you send out. Okay now, do you really need a press clipping bureau? This depends on what you plan to do with the clippings. Public relations firms need this service because it is one of the few methods they have of showing the client what they have accomplished. If it is your own company you are promoting, do you need this proof? It's always nice to see your name in the media, but unless you use these press clippings in some worthwhile merchandising and promotion scheme, it may be a waste of money. Believe me, it does cost money. Just what the rates are depends on the service you hire and the service you need. Here are some of the more important press clipping services. If you are interested, write to them for their latest prices. The promotional material they send you explains exactly what they offer and how much it costs.

American Press Clipping Service   (212)962-3797
119 Nassau Street
New York, NY 10038

ATP Clipping Bureau, Inc.   (212)349-1177
5 Beekman Street
New York, N Y 10038

Bacon's Clipping Bureau   (800)621-0561
14 East Jackson Blvd.
Chicago, IL 60604

Burrelle's Press Clipping Service   (201)992-6600
75 E. Northfield Avenue   (212)227-5570
Livingston, NJ 07039

International Press Clipping Bureau   (212)267-5450
5 Beekman Street
New York, NY 10038

Luce Press Clipping, Inc.   (212)889-6711
420 Lexington Avenue
New York, NY 10017

PUBLICITY NEEDS HUMAN RESOURCES IT CAN CALL ITS OWN

Publicity is a very jealous business. It requires a lot of attention. If it is your own small business, you must provide all the attention. Even if you have a large staff, however, your role is a key one.

There are no formulas for organizing your human resources to give you maximum results. You should set them up to meet your very specific needs. I have worked for and with many different companies. Each had a unique organization. In each case it worked well for them. If it didn't, they changed it. You should, too. There is only one common denominator in all publicity organizations: someone has to be in charge.

The following are basic methods for developing a publicity department. You might want to follow one method exactly, or you might combine several different methods.

When You Work Alone

In a one-person operation, there's no question about who's in charge. If it's your business, you're in charge. You are the decision maker; you are the coordinator. The entire publicity program is your responsibility. Maybe you decide on the easy and expensive way: hire a professional. You are still the one in charge, and don't forget it. If you don't take the responsibility, you'll learn a mighty expensive lesson.

In this situation not only will you make publicity and public relations decisions, but you will contact the media, send out the news releases, and appear on television and radio interview shows yourself. You are it.

When You Have Someone to Assist You

It's a big help if you have someone to handle the details. This person might be someone who is trained or particularly well qualified to conceive, write, rewrite, and follow through to completion specific publicity projects. On the other hand, a talented and interested amateur—a family member, friend, or secretary—can quickly learn the ropes of contacting the media, "selling" a story, arranging for television and radio interviews, and getting out the mailings.

Still, you must be in charge. You must guide day-to-day operations to make sure they remain in line with your goals.

"Media Experts" May Be Your Best Solution

Many large companies find this to be the most effective organizational method. It is also a good method for someone just starting out because it is easier for a beginner to specialize in one medium than to try to cover everything.

Say you put someone in charge of making all the television and radio contacts and of booking company officials on specific shows. The advantage is that in less time they can learn who is in charge of interview shows, take more time to study the needs and requirements of certain shows, and aim the interviewee and subject to meet those needs.

Your job is to coordinate the work done by the television and radio person with that done by the person specializing in newspapers, magazines, or trade publications.

Department Heads Can Be in Charge of Their Own Publicity

If your company has more than one product or service or if for any reason your company is divided into separate functions, you might consider placing each department head in charge of the publicity for his or her own section while you remain responsible for coordinating the publicity from all departments.

Some Companies Organize Around Corporatewide Services

This public relations setup is generally feasible only for a much larger company or a corporation, but you might find it helpful in devising your own plan. In this instance, there is a director of publicity, an assistant director, and managers of corporate news, product news, publications, special events, and stockholder relations.

HOW JOHN DIGGS GETS STARTED

Come on, now. You didn't really expect John Diggs to get all his publicity by himself, now did you? Let's face it, he has a company to run.

What's he to do? Hire a professional? After all, the goals he has set, the means of achieving those goals, are more than an amateur can handle. Right? Wrong.

John Diggs has to start someplace. He does this by setting up a publicity department within his office.

John Diggs Supplies His Publicity Office

Since he's a big shot, John Diggs doesn't furnish the office and stock it himself. He has an assistant to do this. Before the assistant is finished, the new Diggs Shovel Company publicity office is equipped with the newest and fastest word-processing equipment, plenty of desks and files, telephones, and stationery and office supplies, right down to the last paper clip. He's ready to move.

John Diggs Sets up His Publicity Support System

Because he plans to get out large national mailings and because he doesn't yet know how much of the job his own staff will be able to handle, John Diggs checks out all the services available to publicity people: multiple copy services, photo labs, mailing services, professional photographers, temporary office employees, a telephone answering service, and even press clipping services since he may want to use the results of his publicity for promotional materials.

John Diggs Staffs His Publicity Office

Setting up the office space is of prime importance, but offices don't do publicity, people do. Where will John Diggs get his publicity people?

He has decided to use people from his own company and train them. They don't have any more experience than you do, but he's going to let them learn on the job, just as he will.

First, he has decided against forming a permanent publicity staff. He plans to draw employees from different departments to work only when they are needed or to have them spend only a limited number of hours in their publicity efforts. When they work on publicity, they do that work in the publicity office. It is still the hub of the operation.

John Diggs Decides to Train "Specialists"

Instead of having several people working on all facets of the publicity program, possibly at cross-purposes, John Diggs has decided to assign one person to handle each of several specialities. This is a combination of media specialists and corporate specialists. These specialities include television and radio, consumer print media, trade publications, special events, and photography.

By allowing each individual to specialize, he believes they will learn their special function faster and better. As each becomes well-versed in his or her own field, John Diggs considers shifting them around so that, ultimately, each of them is able to handle all functions. This, of course, gives him the opportunity of changing his organizational setup if circumstances warrant it.

Because the goals John Diggs has formulated for his company are so all-encompassing, he considers having one person assigned to each goal, just as many public relations firms have account executives. It is their job to conceive of overall publicity plans to reach these goals and to coordinate media coverage to achieve those goals.

These goal tenders report back to John Diggs, who is the ultimate decision maker and coordinator and who has the final responsibility.

John Diggs Meets With His Publicity Staff

With office and staff in place, John Diggs can now begin the actual publicity. He sets up a meeting with his goal tenders and media specialists, and they decide whether to concentrate on one goal or tackle all goals at the same time. They decide in the beginning to concentrate on only one objective. This is subject to change when the program is underway.

Media Specialists Are Given Assignments

Having spent their preliminary time learning something about the media to which they have been assigned, these media specialists now work with the goal tender in charge to obtain the most valuable target-oriented coverage possible. Once armed with both their own media information and the public relations target, they each come up with a plan of operation, collect the research information they need to tell a specific goal-oriented story, and, finally, get the publicity underway.

CHAPTER PERSPECTIVE

This chapter showed you how to structure your publicity organization to obtain the maximum efficiency from your office space, how to establish your support system of outside services, and how to tap your available human resources. As you continue through this book, you will see how important it is to lay down the proper foundation before undertaking the more creative side of publicity.

How to Spot News in Your Company

INTRODUCTION AND MAIN POINTS

In this chapter we will show you how every company, from the smallest to the largest, has news to report. We will discuss why each news story is another method of selling your product or service, and we will point out how news stories affect both the sale of your product and the image of your company.

After studying the material in this chapter:

■ You will learn what makes a story news to the greatest number of people.

■ You will learn how to make your company news work for you and the sale of your product or service.

■ You will be able to uncover and identify all sorts of news in your company.

■ You will learn what basic information you need to prepare a news release.

After turning in to the copydesk a story I had picked up at the police station, which was on my beat, I was ready to toss in the towel for the day. Then Duke LaRue, the copy chief, a tough old ex-Hearst copy editor, said, "When I was a reporter, we'd turn in ten . . . fifteen stories a day. Now, one story and you kids call it a day."

I was just a cub reporter, but I had been challenged. The gauntlet had been thrown down. I picked it up. I said, "I'll bet I can turn in fifteen stories in one day."

Duke just laughed, unpleasantly, and went back to work. I was effectively dismissed.

The next day after covering my own beats—the police station, fire department, and board of education—more thoroughly than I ever had before, I began pestering everyone I could for additional news items. I raided everyone else's beats, in person and on the phone, to get stories that other reporters had missed. By the time I was finished, I had sixteen news stories, most of them only one paragraph long, but they were news stories. One of the stories was picked up by the Associated Press.

This one experience was better than anything I had learned to date. It taught me that there is news everywhere, just begging to be reported. It also taught me that the best news rarely comes up and bites you. You sometimes have to ask questions until the real news reveals itself.

At that time I was just as much an amateur at this news reporting business as you may be, which only goes to prove that although it may take awhile, you, too, can learn to spot the news in your company—among your personnel and about your products and services. The stories don't have to be long, complicated, or earth-shattering. As I discovered, sometimes short anecdotes are the most interesting and they make wonderful and convenient fillers for all sorts of editors.

PUBLICITY IS REPORTING THE NEWS

Some of your best publicity comes down to one thing: reporting the news. If you can keep this in mind as you tackle publicity for your company, your product, or your service, you can get publicity whenever or wherever you need it. It may be that you create the news you report, but we deal with that in a later chapter. In this chapter we concentrate on finding and reporting the already existing news in your company.

EVERY HEALTHY COMPANY NATURALLY GENERATES NEWS

Any active, growing company continually changes. Change is what news is all about. Just the ordinary, everyday functions of running a company often make news. You hire or promote someone—news. You add a new storefront—news. You renovate, redecorate, or expand—news. You relocate—news. You develop a new product—big news! You improve your product—news again. You make an acquisition or buy a new franchise—news. You have an increase in sales or earnings—financial news. You produce new sales literature or in-store or point-of-purchase displays—business news. You begin a new advertising or promotion campaign—again, business news.

Just how important the news is, and to whom, depends on the type and importance of your company, the importance of the news, and the importance of the individuals involved. Yet, even small changes are news to someone.

It's true that a small change won't make as big a splash in the media as your new product probably made; nevertheless, it can make a few waves. Business editors of all media like to keep up with these things, especially if your business is in an economically influential industry. Certainly the editors of the trade publications in your field of interest want to know what you're doing. They may not have the space to print all the new things that you plan, particularly if you're a promotionally busy company, but the very fact that your company is promotionally active might make a feature story reporting all your promotional activities and your promotional philosophy, a case study of what you are doing, why you are doing it, and whether or not (and how much) it helps increase your sales.

ALL RIGHT THEN, WHAT EXACTLY IS NEWS?

When environmentalists informed the public that dolphins were being injured and killed in the nets used for catching tuna, companies that use tuna in their products were directly affected. This quickly became a serious public relations problem for them. What could they do?

Alpo Petfoods led the way by becoming "the first major pet food manufacturer to ensure that its products contain only tuna caught by methods unharmful to dolphins."

This was news.

If you are going to get your company, product, or service mentioned in the editorial columns of any publication or electronic medium, you must first learn what constitutes news. There is no single definition. Many things make news. It is also true that what may seem to be news to one person isn't news at all to someone else.

When it comes to product and company promotion, it is often the case that a company's news is only so to the company. It is when your news affects someone else's life or business that it becomes news to them. Therefore, always try to make your news relevant to someone else as well.

Now, keep in mind that unless that "somebody" can and will buy your product, or influence others to buy it, news doesn't do your sales figures a bit of good. It is better to get a particle of news to a handful of potential customers than a big story that doesn't increase sales. This is especially true for industrial and farm products, for which the general public is rarely the audience a manufacturer needs to reach.

Learn to Think Like an Editor

Each day editors decide what is news for his or her publication, television, or radio show. Each editor looks for something different and weighs each available story, keeping in mind that each audience is different and learns to expect certain things from each particular medium. Editors judge your press release or news tips on the basis of what their public wants to read, see, or hear, not on the basis of what you or anyone else might want them to print.

There are at least three considerations any good editor weighs when making a decision:

1. Is it timely?
2. Did it happen nearby?
3. Is it about someone or something of interest to my readers, viewers, or listeners?

What Is Timely Is News

News has a short life span, so report it immediately. With the electronic media, the life span of news has become even shorter. What happens right now is more newsworthy than what happened fifteen minutes ago; what happened fifteen minutes ago is more newsworthy than what happened two hours ago; what happened today is more newsworthy than what happened yesterday, and so on. Many companies ignore the news in their organizations until it is no longer news.

You may argue that many feature stories report what happened not only last month but last year and even many years ago. True, but look at the lead paragraph once again. In almost every instance, even in a feature story that doesn't depend particularly on timeliness to grab space, you see some reference to the news, some reason the media selected this particular date to run a particular story. It may be a legal holiday, a national or a community anniversary, or perhaps the birthday of some important historical personality.

What Happens Nearby Is News

What is news to some is not necessarily news to others. Often it is a matter of proximity. Let me put it this way: if there is a fire in your building, this is news to you. On the other hand, if there is a fire in a building in the next town, it is probably news only to the people in that town.

News Is of Interest to a Particular Audience

"Nearby" may be thought of in a broader sense. It can also mean that the news strikes close to home—"hits you where you live." News may also be something of local interest, like your high school football game, or it might be of national interest, such as the NFL Championship Playoff Game. Anyone interested in football is probably interested in both. This also refers to interest groups. Reaching these people means saying something of specific interest to engineers in an engineering journal or reporting something of importance to the farm community or the ecologically interested community: "A safe new chemical compound that will cut farm costs in half has been introduced to the market by . . . ."

The More News Elements the Better

Keep in mind that the more news elements you have in a given story, the more likely it is to be picked up by the media. Just one of the following news essentials might not be enough, whereas a combination of several might even give you a national story.

1. You have hired a new chef for your restaurant.
2. The new chef you have hired was the chef for a famous television personality.
3. The chef has a very famous specialty, one so popular it has been named after him.

Train Yourself and Your Personnel to Be on the Lookout for News

Before you can spot news, however, it is essential that you know precisely what to look for. Before we get into the details, it might help you to have a simple checklist that you can tack up on bulletin boards to keep employees alerted as to what news really is and what they should look for in the way of news.

A NEW OR IMPROVED PRODUCT
■ A new product
■ An improved product

This is possibly the most important news your company can have. If you don't have a product or a service to sell, you don't have a business. Each time you come out with a new product and each time you improve your product, you have an important news story. Potential customers, as well as editors, want a description of the new or improved product, an explanation of what the product is for, how it is used, why the product was invented or improved, and the cost. Other interesting facts for your news release include how long the new or improved product has been in the making, in what way it is different, and the market this product is intended to reach. Specify whether you plan to introduce the product nationwide or in a specific geographic market, and describe your advertising and promotional plans to support the introduction of the new product.

PROMOTIONS AND APPOINTMENTS
- A new executive
- Promoted personnel

One of your company's most valuable assets is its people. When you promote or appoint someone to a position in your company, it gives you the opportunity to tell your potential customers that your products and services are backed up by the best people in the business. Editors want to know who has been elected, appointed, or promoted to what position, and why. They want to know the employee's past accomplishments and new responsibilities, any previous positions or titles, and previous company affiliations, as well as whom he or she is replacing. Include a photograph of the individual featured in the story, preferably a head shot.

YOU RETAIN A NEW OUTSIDE SERVICE
- A new distributor
- A new sales representative
- A new importer or exporter
- A company to conduct a survey
- A new sales promotion firm
- A new advertising agency

An outside service is always a sales advantage. Each time you retain an outside service, you expand the effectiveness, reputation, and image of your company, as well as your services to your clients. You should provide the exact name of the company you have retained, along with the location of the home office. If you retain one branch of the company, say so. Specify. If you know the name of the person who will be in charge of your account, give that person's name and title. Now, specify precisely what the new outside service or agency is expected to accomplish, precisely what their duties will be. If their duties are limited to a particular territory, be sure to specify what that territory is, geographically. If the territory is determined by any other factors, identify those factors.

A NEW SERVICE
- A faster delivery service
- New educational services
- A new 800 telephone number

All other things being equal, a service offered by your company can make the difference between a sale and no sale. This is particularly true in a depressed economy when many customers shop for better service as well as better prices. If you have added a new service, specify the nature of the service, what it is expected to do, and whom it is set up to help. Is it nationwide or limited by territory? When does it go into effect? How long will it be in effect? What need triggered this new service? Why will this service be of importance to your customers?

NEW CAMPAIGNS
- A new advertising campaign
- A new publicity campaign
- A new sales promotion campaign
- A new merchandising program

When you get publicity for your advertising or promotional campaign, you maximize the dollar spent on these campaigns. Regardless of the type of campaign you prepare you need to explain precisely what sort of campaign it is and to whom it is targeted. If there is a theme, state it. Who is in charge of the campaign? When will it begin? If newspapers, television, radio, or trade publications are involved, be sure to find out which, where, and why. Explain what triggered the need for this campaign. Many publications like to know the amount of money budgeted for the campaign, as well as where and how it will be spent.

NEW MERCHANDISING

- A new dealer promotion
- New sales or promotional literature
- New point-of-purchase items
- A new offer
- A contest
- A new catalog

Merchandising and sales promotion presell the customer and the customer's customer, and they educate the customer. If you release any new sales promotion materials, explain what they are and toward whom they are targeted. Describe any literature and the message it is meant to convey. Describe any offer, contest, or catalog. Define those who will receive the literature, and state precisely who is eligible to participate in the contests. Explain how your customers and potential customers can enter their names to take advantage of your merchandising plans. When will it begin? How will it begin? Are there advertising and promotional plans to back it up?

CHANGING THE COMPANY OR PRODUCT IMAGE

- A new product design
- A new trademark
- A new package or package design
- A new logo
- A company name change

In addition to sending the media copies of the new design, be sure to explain why you selected this specific design. Go into detail. Designs help create the image you desire for your company and your products or services. Are you introducing a new trademark, or even a new logo? Provide a good professional photograph of the new design. Provide background on the design: why was a new design needed at this time? Why was this particular design selected from perhaps dozens of other designs? Point out special features of the design. Try to get a verbal description of the design by the head of the design department or from the person who created the design. Make a note of the designer's thought processes as he or she created the design. This is especially interesting to the media. For most of this you need to interview the CEO, the design director, and even the individual who created the design. (Obtain the instructions handed to the designers regarding the ultimate effect the design is to create.) If it is a trademark design, ask how and where it will be applied. Will it be as effective in black and white as in color? Are there special features? What image is it designed to convey? If it is a new package design, is it a new surface design or an entirely new package package design? What are the new features? Why were they considered important? Is it a new product design? Why? When will the new design be seen on the shelves or by the public? Where will it be seen? Will there be a massive promotional or advertising campaign to introduce the new design? If so, when does this begin?

AN EXAMPLE OF COMPANY GROWTH

- A new showroom
- A new branch
- A new office
- A new dealer
- A new franchise
- A new subsidiary
- A new division

The media like to know when a company is growing and healthy. Be specific about the new expansion: what it is, where it is, who is in charge, how it came about, plans for it, and how it relates to the parent company.

NEW OR IMPROVED FACILITIES

- Business relocation
- Plant modernization
- Plant expansion
- Redecoration or renovation
- Construction of a new facility

This sort of concrete evidence of a growing company is good news to report. Explain what exactly is being done and why, where it is being done, when it will begin, how long it will take, who is in charge, when the work will be completed, when you will move in, and on what date your customers will be able to reach you there. If you are planning special events, promotion, or advertising to announce the completion of the project, be specific.

NEW MARKETS

- Going after new market segments
- Entering a new market

━ An expanded market
━ A new market segment

Information you need includes the market you are going after, a statement of the markets you are currently in, why the new market is important, why you decided to target this specific market, the means by which you plan to sell, and whether you plan to change your product or service in any way to more closely meet the needs of the new market.

RESEARCH

━ New research plans
━ A technological breakthrough

Everyone is interested in new research plans and developments, especially if that research might affect their future. Get a statement from the research director about the nature of the research or the technological breakthrough, what the new research is expected to accomplish, or what the technological breakthrough means to the future of your company, the industry, the community, the nation, and the world. Obtain the name and title of the director of the research and development department and the names of those assigned to this particular project.

YOU BEGIN OR COMPLETE A PROJECT

━ Signing a big contract
━ An important and successful installation

Editors and readers like case histories. Begin when you sign the contract to keep careful notes, and if a photograph might tell the story a bit better, take one and keep it in your files. Date everything so that when you are ready to prepare the case history for a trade publication, you can explain everything in chronological order.

POCKETBOOK ISSUES

━ A price change
━ An unusual sale

Why are prices being lowered or raised, and by how much? When does the price change go into effect? Who will be affected by this price change? If it bodes well for the company or industry, stress this. If this follows the industry trend or an economic trend, mention it. Report anything that has been done to the product or service that explains the price change.

YOUR COMPANY'S ANNUAL SHAREHOLDERS MEETING
- A new appointment to the board of directors
- Annual meetings of shareholders

These should be monitored carefully. You need the proxy statement, including the issues to be voted on, such as the election of directors, stock options, and reappointment of auditors, and any other news of interest to shareholders.

FINANCIAL STATEMENTS
- A company merger or acquisition
- Company financing

Report what sort of transaction it is, specify the type of and reasons for the transaction you are planning and who is making the first move, and explain the details of the negotiations.

YOUR SALES AND EARNINGS
- Your earnings report
- A sales increase

If you are a reporting company, you are expected to report earnings per share and net income and revenue or sales. Although a private company is not required to divulge sales and earnings, it may be to your advantage to do so.

STOCK INFORMATION
- Announcement of a dividend
- Announcement of a stock split

You must specify what you are offering: a dividend or a stock split. If you announce a dividend, you should report the amount of the dividend, if there has been a previous dividend and, if so, the amount. State how the new dividend is to be paid: the frequency, the date the checks will be mailed, and precisely which shareholders are entitled to the dividend, e.g., "Payable to shareholders of record on (date)." If you announce a stock split, be sure to report the exact split and how many shares will be outstanding after the stock dividend is paid. Also explain how the stock dividend or split affects any other current cash dividends.

A CAPITAL INVESTMENT
- New manufacturing equipment
- New technical equipment

Precisely what is the new equipment? Why is it needed? Is it on the "cutting edge" of new technology? Is it merely a replacement or a step forward in an overall updating of your plant? Who bought the new equipment? What department is it for? Precisely what does it do that the old equipment did not do? What is the cost? Will it lower production costs?

PUBLIC APPEARANCES
- A speech
- Appearances on television and radio
- Trade show activities

Every public appearance gives the speaker an opportunity to say something quotable for the press. Include in your press release any statement that is newsworthy and timely. Predictions and forecasts also make good news copy. You need the name of the speaker, title, the company he or she represents, the formal title of the group addressed, and salient points of the speech. You must be sure to specify when and where the speech was made. It is helpful to have the full text of the speech available to give to the media.

MEETINGS
- Sales meetings
- Annual meetings

What is the purpose of the meeting? Where and when will it be held? Name who will be at the meeting: by company, job titles, and duties. How many will attend? How long will it last? Who will be in charge of the meeting? Are there to be speeches? Who will give these speeches? Be sure to get names, addresses, affiliated companies, affiliated organizations, subjects of speeches, and why individuals were selected to speak. Try to get advance copies of the agenda and all speeches or, at the very least, important and timely excerpts from the speeches.

ANNIVERSARIES
- A company anniversary
- A product anniversary
- The length of time you have been in a community

If it is an anniversary, describe the occasion. Which anniversary (number of years)? How do you plan to observe the anniversary? Will it be a private event, a companywide event, a community event, or perhaps a national event? When will the event be held? Who is invited? From how far away are guests coming? Obtain a list of important guests.

SPECIAL EVENTS
- Previews
- A groundbreaking
- An open house
- A plant tour
- A special exhibit

What type of special event is it? When is it being held? Why is it being held? What do you hope to accomplish? Are you aiming at a special-interest group? Who? What? What is special about the event? Obtain background material on whatever it is that prompted the event.

RECORDS
- A sales record
- A record production for a day, week, or year
- The "first" off the production line
- The "most" of almost anything
- The largest order
- The largest installation

Records mark the unusual, and anything unusual is newsworthy. Has any department in your company set a record for something: production, sales, or attendance? Who set the past record? Who broke the record—the company or a person in your company? Be sure to find out names, jobs, titles, and home addresses. Take a photograph of one or all of the record breakers. If the record is for something particularly interesting, take a picture of the individual or group doing whatever it was they did to break the record. Obtain quotes from participants to reveal the excitement and enthusiasm of the event. How long ago was the original record set? Was it set by your company or another company, is the same individual breaking his or her own record, or is someone in your company breaking another's record? Be specific.

AWARDS
- To an employee
- To someone outside your company
- To your company

For community service

Recognition means someone or something is outstanding. Editors like to know about outstanding people and events. Who received the award? Describe the award to be given. What is the award for? When will the award be presented? Will the event be special—a dinner or a special public presentation? List important guests.

PERSONAL MILESTONES

- An employee's retirement
- An employee anniversary
- Birth
- Marriage
- The anniversary of an old-timer

You might have a news collection box, much like the traditional suggestion box, into which individuals can drop personal or office news items. Give them a guideline of what to look for and what information to provide: the name of the person and nature of the news, home address, date of event, information about his or her family.

EMPLOYEE ACTIVITIES

- An employee's unusual hobby
- Employee parties
- Employee organizations

If the story is about someone who has an unusual hobby, try to get a photograph showing that person involved in the hobby. Announce all employee parties and employee organization meetings. If solid news emanates from them, report it.

CHAPTER PERSPECTIVE

This chapter helped you identify and report the news in your company to keep your company name and its products before the public. To be successful in obtaining ongoing publicity for your company, you must become adept at spotting and reporting every bit of business and social news throughout every department. The next chapter will explain how you can take this basic information and turn it into professional news releases.

Writing the News Release

INTRODUCTION AND MAIN POINTS

In this chapter we will introduce you to the art of writing a news release, as well as explain why this is so important in obtaining publicity for your business. We will give you tips for selecting the proper information for each paragraph and we will focus on the details necessary to make your press release as professional as possible. We will also provide you with a sample news release sent out by John Diggs.

After studying the material in this chapter:

■ You will learn what information goes in the lead paragraph.

■ You will discover how to summarize your latest news.

■ You will learn how to give facts in order of importance.

■ You will learn the best methods for identifying personnel, companies and events.

■ You will acquire methods for keeping news releases short.

■ You will learn techniques for making every news release sell.

Writing a news release is a bit like recording a conversation with a knowledgeable and interested friend. Your friend asks, "Anything new at your company?"

You'd probably answer, "Steve Connors just got promoted to marketing director."

Interested, your friend would probably ask, "What was his former job?"

You'd respond, "He was the sales manager."

"Ummm," your friend says. "What are his new responsibilities?"

"He's going to be in charge of sales and marketing, including advertising and sales promotion."

Now, put this together into a press release:

FOR IMMEDIATE RELEASE

Steven J. Connors has been named marketing director for the Omni Corporation in Davenport, Iowa, according to John Reisdale, President.

Formerly sales manager for the company, Connors will now be responsible for long-range advertising and public relations planning.

You probably add other credentials, perhaps a statement from Mr. Connors about his plans or goals or a statement from the president regarding Mr. Connor's past achievements.

APPLY THE SAME TECHNIQUE TO ALL COMPANY NEWS

You can apply the same technique to almost any news about your company. You don't even need someone to ask you the leading questions—ask them of yourself. When you ask yourself, "Anything new at your company?" you might answer,

We're merging with the Juniper Company.
We're launching a new product next month.
We're planning a big promotion for our fiftieth anniversary.

Listen to yourself the next time someone asks, "What's new?" Then notice how, after you've given them the highlights in your first sentence, they ask for the most important, the most pertinent, facts first. Then they ask for the next most important information.

Knowledgeable people ask questions in the form of an inverted pyramid. They generally want the latest news first, so you provide them in conversation and in your news release with the climax first: expand it a bit, and then go back to the beginning and give the details. This is the way news stories are formed, as well. It's a logical progression. In a news release you provide the information in the same order as the questions come to the mind of the reader.

THE FIRST PARAGRAPH SUMMARIZES THE LATEST NEWS

In a continuing or developing story in which the final result is unknown, it is the latest news or most recent development that is reported in the lead paragraph. For example, the answers to these questions constitute a lead paragraph:

What's the latest on the merger?

Have you launched your new product yet?

What have you planned for your fiftieth anniversary?

What were your earnings for this quarter?

When will your new sales promotion materials be available?

Where will you be advertising?

When will your first advertising run on television?

When will your new building be finished?

Are you planning a ground-breaking ceremony?

Have you finished moving into your new offices?

NOW, GIVE THEM THE DETAILS IN ORDER OF IMPORTANCE

The paragraphs following the first paragraph are called the body of the story. Use these paragraphs to explain and expand on the points you made in the lead. Try to include details in the order of their interest and value, just as you would in explaining them to a friend.

For an appointment or promotion, these additional facts or details might include the following:

▬ Specify why this person was selected for the job.

▬ List the responsibilities of the position.

▬ Explain past experience that qualifies him or her for the job.

▬ Include remarks by the spokesperson.

When a new outside service has been retained:

▬ Specify the type of outside service retained.

▬ Define territories and responsibilities.

When you announce a new campaign:

▬ Select the major thrust of the advertising campaign.

▬ Explain the type of campaign.

▬ Explain what you hope to accomplish: the target.

▬ State when the campaign or promotion begins.

▬ State how the promotion will operate.

▬ List the advertising or promotional backup.

If you are coming out with new promotional materials:

▬ Explain the type of new materials.

▬ Describe the new promotional materials.

▬ Discuss the cost.

▬ Explain how to obtain the new materials.

▬ Discuss their uses.

▬ Explain when, how, and where they will be available.

If you plan changes in your facilities:
- Explain why you are moving, building, or renovating.
- Report what you will be doing and when.
- State who is in charge.
- Announce the anticipated completion date of the project.

Financial news takes considerable explanation:
- Report the type of transaction.
- Explain details of the negotiations.
- Give reasons for the transaction.

How Persons Are Identified

Persons are identified ordinarily by their names, addresses, occupations, current or former titles or distinctions, ages, or connections with the story in hand. Use full names, correct initials, addresses, and titles: John E. Smith, President of the XYZ Company, Dayton, Ohio. Stress their business experience because this is why he or she can contribute to your company and your business. Why this particular person? Does he have a strong background in research and development, engineering, production, or service-related skills? If so, say so. Is her strength in management skills? Mention it. Has someone from a target market been added to the staff? Be sure the targeted market segment knows this because it indicates that your company is fully prepared to handle their type of business efficiently.

Make Sure Names Are Spelled Correctly

Don't just take a stab at the spelling of names—check. Read them back to the person being written about. Check the spelling with them. If the initials are W.B., don't assume that the "W" stands for William. It may be Walter or Wilhelm. Make sure the middle initial is "B." A "B" sounds a lot like "D." And check the spelling of the names. Is it John or Jon? Is it Mary or Mari? Is it Joan or Joanne? People often choose a name with an unusual spelling, and they may be offended by a misspelling. When a name is spelled incorrectly, it shows carelessness, of course, but it may also be interpreted as disrespect. Moreover, it is simply bad reporting. When in doubt, check with the person who knows, the person whose name or whose hometown it is.

How Companies Are Identified

A company may be identified in relation to an industry, type of products or services offered, how long it has been in business, and where it is located.

In identifying a company, it is also important to make sure that the name of the company today is the same as it was yesterday. Not only are acquisitions and mergers continually changing things, but so too are companies that incorporate or that simply want to change their image and use a name change as part of that image-changing effort.

How Events Are Identified

You can identify an event by its purpose, its relation to anniversaries or other significant events, and its sponsor.

KEEP YOUR SENTENCES SHORT AND SIMPLE

Try to keep each sentence in your press release twenty words or less. Although twenty words usually takes up less than two lines of typed copy, it takes more than one-half inch of space when packed in a narrow newspaper column. Look at your own newspaper. Notice how much easier it is to read a short sentence than it is to read a long one. Try the same experiment with paragraphs of differing lengths. If this doesn't help you remember to keep your sentences and paragraphs short, nothing will.

Here are several methods for keeping sentences short and simple:

▬ Omit extraneous adjectives and other words—but not important facts.

▬ Use declarative sentences: "The Omni Company is celebrating its fiftieth anniversary this year, according to . . . ."

▬ Eliminate dependent clauses and phrases: "The Omni Company, *which is observing its 50th anniversary this year* . . . ."

▬ Instead of using "and" or "but" in your press release copy, consider using a period or a semicolon.

KEEP YOUR PARAGRAPHS SHORT

Note from reading your own newspaper that there are rarely more than two sentences in any paragraph. It is even better, especially in the lead, to have only one sentence. In the body of the story, use a new paragraph for each separate point.

This makes it easier for the editor to rearrange the paragraphs without changing the sense of the copy and allows the editor to cut paragraphs to fit available news column space. Incidentally, just so you'll keep the most important information near the top of the press release, remember that editors cut from the bottom.

It is easier for some to use 3 × 5 index cards to organize information:

■ On a 3 × 5 card, write one point that you want to make in each paragraph.

■ Under each topic, list everything directly related to that subject.

■ Write one paragraph around each point. If the paragraph is too long, cut it or rewrite until it contains no more than four sentences, each sentence twenty words or less.

■ Arrange your cards in order of importance.

KEEP YOUR PRESS RELEASE AS BRIEF AS POSSIBLE

Just because a bonafide newspaper reporter can get a full column for a story, you can't command that much space. Unless the news is of extreme importance, condense your double-spaced news release to one page or less. This should be under 200 words. Since trade publications require more information than a newspaper, however, the story can be longer if the pertinent facts require it.

CHOOSE FAMILIAR WORDS

The words that are familiar to a college professor may not be familiar to a police officer, and vice versa. The technical terms, figures, or unusual names that are familiar to the engineer may not be understood by the CEO. However, since you are writing for more than one type of reader, you should strive to use the language that every reader understands. This certainly does not mean talking down to your readers: it means translating the technical and buzzwords into everyday language, or at least providing an adequate explanation.

If technical terms must be used or if figures, unusual names, or places are essential to the meaning of the story, it is important for purposes of clarity to keep your sentences as short as possible, even shorter than the twenty words previously suggested.

If the technical terms are unfamiliar to you, you should double-check their spelling and proper usage. Remember, though, ordinary words can often be just as tricky. Whenever there is a question about how even a simple word should be spelled, look it up. This is what dictionaries are for.

MAKE EVERY NEWS RELEASE SELL

In reading about a political figure recently, I learned how he was "rehearsed" for a debate. Regardless of the subject or question posed by the opponent, the politician was rehearsed to respond to the charge or answer the question quickly and then get back to the basic message.

In your case you always begin with some subject of interest to the media—news—and then get back to your basic message, selling your product or service.

Imagine you announce that you have hired someone of importance for a key position in your company. The announcement is the news vehicle. It should include the who, what, when, where, and how required by every news release, but the "why" carries the basic message.

How many times have you seen the "why" left out of a personnel announcement—and wondered about it? Surely, not every personnel change is political, nor is everyone promoted the son or daughter of the boss. In most instances, there is an important "why." The person probably offered your company and your customers a sound "why." Find out what it is, and highlight it in your news announcement.

Give this statment considerable thought. "We think he is a fine fellow" just isn't enough. It is certainly not the reason he was hired or promoted. If you hired or promoted someone to give the customer better service, say so. If this is the case, this becomes your basic message.

When confronted with a news story, the reader always wants to know,"How does this affect me or my company? What can I get out of this?." Answer these questions to the reader's satisfaction, and you have a potential customer.

CONCENTRATE ON YOUR BASIC SALES MESSAGE

You may not be tops in all categories, but you won't be in business long if you aren't tops in at least one. This becomes your basic sales message. If you have two or more, great; use them—one at a time.

- Our product is superior.
- Our service is superior.
- Our company is a superior source.
- We have top-notch people.
- We have the best prices.
- We have the best promotional support system.

Report Why Your Product Is Superior

Your customers and potential customers would be impressed to know that someone has been added to your staff with the following responsibilities:
- Quality control
- Stepping up research and development

Report Why Your Service Is Superior

Someone has been hired or promoted to improve the following areas:
- Distributor coverage
- Customer service
- The dealer advertising and identification program
- Personnel training
- Channeling of internal information for clients
- Servicing of distributor accounts
- Supervising of dealer relations
- Processing and expediting of wholesale orders
- Creating store special events for company clients

Potential customers like to know that special attention will be given to their specific geographic needs. Consider these "why" statements:
- The company is opening a new regional office in Atlanta.
- He is the new western regional sales manager.
- She will be responsible for the Pacific Northwest area.
- He is responsible for sales, marketing, and customer services for the entire Eastern Seaboard.

Consider including a statement from the newly hired or promoted person that outlines what he or she plans to accomplish—what he or she plans to do for the customer:

My goal is to reduce delivery time by days—not just hours.

I plan to keep in closer touch with our customers so that we are in a better position to take care of their immediate needs.

Report Why Your Company Is a Superior Source

The image of your company in the eyes of decision makers, as well as the financial public, is important. People like to deal with a good, reliable firm. It may be that your company is a good neighbor, size may be the factor, and growth and expansion are important:

"This new facility," stressed (name), "will enable us to be more competitive—with the accent on service and delivery, which are the most important factors in the (type of) market."

Our Company announces an expansion move to increase the distribution of (type of) supplies in the Pacific Northwest.

Our Company has opened a new 0000 sq. ft. showroom in (city/state) geared toward providing better service to the (type of) trade in (city/state).

The new site is ideally located to serve (market areas), plus being close to transportation services necessary to support Our Company's national and international sales.

Our Company has been a fixture in (city) since 19--, and our purchase of the (name of) building signifies our desire to remain at the location for many years.

The change from tenant to owner will enable us to make long-range plans that will be in the best interests of our customers, employees, and suppliers.

(City) was picked because of the easy access to markets in the surrounding territory and the Eastern Seaboard.

Report Why Your Company Has Superior People

People are the company; therefore, the quality and the experience of those in your company reveal the quality of your company:

(Name) has extensive experience in the XXX aftermarket, and is expected to add a great deal of expertise to the firm's marketing programs.

(Name) will head a team with over 75 combined years of sales experience in the distribution field.

(Name) joined Our Company's operation 00 years ago as an installation apprentice, advancing to journeyman, on to a supervisory capacity, and then into production management.

(Name) is credited with licensing and establishing plants in England, France, Switzerland, South Africa, and Australia.

(Name) has been employed by Our Company for 00 years as regional sales manager. His new position will utilize his extensive sales and marketing experience with both industrial and consumer product lines.

(Name)'s vast experience in the (type of) field will be a certain asset to our company and to the industry at large.

Report Why Your Company Has the Best Prices

This "why" may involve closer distribution points to cut down on shipping charges; research and development may produce less expensive innovations:

In response to economic conditions affecting the (type of) industry, Our Company has redeveloped its retail offerings to include a new dating plan, a new volume price plateau structure, and special price incentives.

Our Company and XXX Company will unite in a promotion to offer a savings of up to $00 for the consumer and to stimulate retail sales during the holiday buying season.

In print, the 00% off means a consumer savings of approximately $0.

Report Why Your Promotional Support System Is Superior

A new program of TV spots, to be launched this month by Our Company, will be run for a three-week period on more than 000 stations in 00 major markets.

The new campaign utilizes television, radio, print media, posters, and direct mail to promote the product.

The theme was suggested by the product's special feature and will be an important part of every merchandising effort, including consumer advertising, exposure on national TV, and direct mail campaign.

The advertising campaign is designed to test the effectiveness of television as a medium to sell this type of product.

It is designed to support customer sales by helping increase customer brand awareness of Our Company's name.

HOW TO TURN YOUR NEWS INTO A PROFESSIONAL PRESS RELEASE

- Use 8½ × 11, 16 to 20 pound white bond paper.
- Type your press release with a black ribbon and standard pica or elite type. If you use a word processor, do not use dot matrix print.
- Use only one side of the paper.
- Allow a 1-inch margin on each side of the page and at the bottom. Leave 4 inches at the top of the first page if your press release is very short or if it runs to more than one page. If there is a choice between using two pages or less space at the top, less space at the top is preferable.
- Double-space your copy.
- Indent the first line of each paragraph five spaces.
- Photostatted or otherwise duplicated copies of a release are acceptable as long as they are clear, sharp, and clean.
- Place the name, address, and telephone number of your company in the upper left-hand corner of the first page. Also give the name of the person to contact for further information.
- Type: FOR RELEASE OCTOBER 15 OR THEREAFTER or FOR IMMEDIATE RELEASE a few spaces above the first paragraph.
- If it is a new product announcement, identify the release as a NEW PRODUCT RELEASE or NEW PRODUCT ANNOUNCEMENT.
- The page number goes in the upper right-hand corner if more than one page is required.
- On those rare occasions when your press release runs more than one page, type "more" at the bottom of each page, except the last page. Always end the press release with # # # or - 0 -.
- On the upper left-hand corner of all pages but the first, use one or two words that identify the press release, so if the pages are inadvertently separated they can be identified.
- Use a paper clip, not a staple, to hold together the pages of your press release.

SAMPLE NEWS RELEASE

The John Diggs Shovel Company
Address:
Telephone Number:
        Contact:

                                (Date)

FOR IMMEDIATE RELEASE

John E. Petersen has been named Sales Promotion Manager of the John Diggs Shovel Company, it was announced today by John Diggs, President.

Petersen, who for ten years has been Marketing Director for Farm Equipment, Inc., will coordinate all sales promotion activities for the company's new Back to Basics program.

Petersen said "My goal is to make the public aware of how our everyday activities of gardening and home maintenance can be altered to improve our total environment."

The John Diggs Shovel Company is one of the oldest companies in the Midwest.

CHAPTER PERSPECTIVE

This chapter stressed the necessity of preparing your press releases in a professional manner so that your news can compete with all the other business news releases on the desks of media editors.

Photographs: Taking Them, Captioning Them, and Mailing Them

INTRODUCTION AND MAIN POINTS

In this chapter we will explain why a good photograph is essential to an effective publicity campaign. We will focus on the ways and means of taking good publicity pictures as well as the most effective methods for presenting them to editors. After studying the material in this chapter:

■ You will be able to plan your own photo sessions.

■ You will understand what goes into a good news photo.

■ You will learn how to make your photos speak for you.

■ You will learn how to improve your photo-taking skills.

■ You will be able to select a good photo background.

■ You will learn how to select the best photographer for your particular job.

■ You will learn what information you need for a caption.

■ You will learn how to write, type, and affix a caption.

■ You will learn how to protect your photos for mailing.

You have a photo opportunity set up for this afternoon. The president of the company will be there, as well as the award recipients. You think you've made all the necessary arrangements: hired a photographer, arranged for a room, and notified everyone about the time and place.

You get there early to make sure everything goes okay. The photographer shows up on time. That's a relief. Then people begin to arrive. The photo session is underway. That is, you think it is until the photographer asks,

"Where do you want the pictures taken?"

Where? Didn't you hire an expert? The photographer is looking at you, awaiting your decision. You scan the room. It's cluttered with chairs, tables, and lamps. Quickly you clear some space. The background is awful, but it will have to do. You ask the participants to move to the spot you've cleared.

Then the photographer's questions begin to pile up:

"Do you want them all in the picture? How do you want the picture set up? Do you want them to do anything?"

If you haven't given any thought to these considerations, you are forced to make decisions on the spot and hope for the best.

This scenario is not all that unusual. It has happened to me. It happens even to the best publicists when they become careless. There is a good way to avoid this happening to you. Anticipate any problems that may arise, and do whatever is necessary to avoid them.

PLAN YOUR PHOTOGRAPHIC SESSIONS CAREFULLY

Whether you own the company and handle your own publicity or have been assigned to manage the publicity for someone else's company, it is your job to make all the arrangements for every photographic session—or photo opportunity, as it is sometimes called. If you are to cover a special event, find out what special activities are scheduled, where, and at what time, and give each participant a copy of the schedule.

This includes lining up the place where the pictures will be taken, notifying everyone who is to be in the pictures of the time and place, hiring professional models if you need them, having all the necessary props available, and, of course, making arrangements for a good photographer.

One of your responsibilities, however, may not be as obvious: planning the photographs.

KNOW WHAT YOU WANT YOUR PICTURES TO SAY

Yes, pictures talk. You bet they do. In fact, given a good picture, you can say more about your company, your product, or your service than you can in any number of words.

If you want to get an idea of just how much a photograph can say, study the photographs in a good newspaper or magazine. Really look at the pictures, and then read the picture captions—they're a team. If it's a really good photograph, you are probably compelled to read the caption.

Now consider the various things you want to say about your company, your product, or your service, and then select one of them. Let's say John Diggs wants to tell the community that he is a good and caring neighbor. One day he receives a letter from a committee that is trying to clean up the city's parks. They state that they need volunteers to weed, rake, plant, paint, and pick up litter. They also need money to purchase paint, rakes, and shovels.

Shovels! When John Diggs reads "shovels," his eyes light up. He immediately goes to the telephone and volunteers not only his time, but also as many shovels as they need. Then along with the committee, he plans a photo opportunity when the shovels are delivered.

Once all the arrangements have been made for the delivery of the shovels, the committee—or the Diggs Shovel Company publicity staff—sends a picture memo to all the local news media informing them of the event and giving them the exact day, date, time, and place where they will be able to get pictures. They are also informed about who will be available for pictures, including John Diggs, the committee, and volunteers who will actually use the shovels.

So what does John Diggs have to plan regarding the photographs? Just some picture ideas for his own photographer and other photographers if they should run out of ideas of their own. Here are some of his picture ideas:

1.   The free Diggs shovels being unloaded from the truck.
2.   John Diggs shows the chairman, members of the committee, and/or the volunteers the proper method for holding and using a shovel.
3.   John Diggs makes the first dig.
4.   A small volunteer perches atop a huge pile of the donated shovels.

Will these photographs get the Diggs message across? You bet they will. Actually, these are just a few of the possible picture ideas that will convey this message. Remember, if John Diggs can come up with ideas for something as ordinary as shovels, you can surely come up with photo ideas for your own products or services.

DON'T FORGET THE PHOTO CAPTIONS!

This morning I saw a fascinating picture of a man driving half a car. I wanted to know the details, but there was no caption. All pictures need captions! I still feel cheated. Either the editor thought the picture told the whole story or it was a "teaser" advertisement. It certainly captured my attention, but that wasn't enough. Advertising can get away with such things as photos without captions, but when it comes to publicity, never, never forget to send a picture caption with every picture.

Captions Require Some Effort

At the appointed day and time, John Diggs shows up in his gardening clothes. Following him is a truckload of new shovels, donated—as the caption informs the readers—by the Diggs Shovel Company.

He has discussed the various picture ideas with his photographer and has agreed to suggestions the photographer has offered. Then there is the problem of the picture caption material. People move in and out of pictures, and each caption should list the exact names, from left to right. Now, John Diggs can't be expected to collect the necessary information for captions while he is personally involved in the pictures himself. So he assigns someone from his staff. Simple, you say. Use the same caption for all the pictures. No way. Keep in mind that every picture has people in it—at least one or two people, perhaps dozens. Well, these people should be named, and they should be named from left to right. Woe be it unto you if you give one person the wrong name or if you spell a name wrong.

This means that someone should be in charge of taking accurate notes for picture captions. You usually see someone, often a reporter or even the photographer, approach each person in the photograph just taken—before they have moved—to get their names and addresses in the proper order. In addition to making sure the names are spelled correctly, you also want to find out if they are committee members or volunteers and any other information that adds to the interest of the story. Remember, there also are opportunities for quotes from grateful committee members.

If you cover a photo setup with your own photographer, and you certainly should, you should assign someone to do the same thing for your photographer, making sure to code each caption with any identifying symbol, usually a number, given you by the photographer. Only in this way can you match caption to photograph once the printed pictures are returned to you.

OBTAIN A PHOTO RELEASE

For legal safety, it's generally a good idea to get a release from each person photographed. It is wise to have everyone appearing in a picture sign a simple form to the effect: Permission to use my name and/or photograph for publicity purposes is hereby given. (Signature)

WHAT MAKES A GOOD PICTURE?

I have found three general rules to be helpful in planning photographs:

1. Take pictures of people doing whatever they normally do in places where they normally do it.
2. Keep the picture as narrow as possible and, if feasible, limit the posed shot to only one person.
3. If more than one subject is essential to a photograph, group them in such a way that the overall shot is as tight and narrow as possible.

You Can Learn A Lot by Studying Published Photos

If you read a daily newspaper or have magazines around the house, you already have some of the best photographic textbooks available. Study the pictures used. Try to figure out why a picture grabs and holds your attention. Is it because it is of a famous personality? Is it the composition of the picture? Is it the expression of someone's face? Is it the action?

Now, tear out a newspaper photograph that has caught your attention. Why did you select this particular newspaper photograph? Can you identify with it? Does it say something to you? Does it have emotional appeal? Is someone doing something interesting?

Editors look long and hard for pictures that have these ingredients. Inject these elements into every publicity picture you take.

Study Good Photographs for the Way Things Should Be Done

Try an experiment. Take out your photograph album, and notice how you took pictures of one person, two people, or a group of people. How are they grouped? What are they doing? Where are they looking? Can you see the faces clearly?

Now, try to find newspaper or magazine pictures with the same number of people. If the picture is posed, note how the photographer handles the situation. How did he or she group the subjects? What are they doing? Where are they looking? Can you see the faces clearly?

Newsphotos are very different from posed publicity shots. In capturing the drama of a news event there may be several inches of empty space between people in a two-column picture. However, note how you rarely find wasted space in a posed photograph. Editors hate wasted space in a photograph. This means that when you photograph a product and a person, or two people or more, keep them close—and I mean close—together. This means shoulders touching or even overlapping. Make sure your photograph can be used in one column. If it can't be trimmed, you've probably cut yourself out of some free publicity.

There are two more rules you should always follow in publicity photographs: keep everything centered so the photograph can be trimmed without destroying the purpose of your picture, and when you photograph a product, make very sure that you photograph the product closely enough that you can see the details, especially any new or important features.

A Good Publicity Picture Is One with Which Readers Can

Editors like pictures of people. Why? Because as human beings, we identify with other human beings. The more like us they tend to be, the more we can identify with them. This extends even to the faces of strangers that have become familiar by repeated exposure on television, in the movies, or even in other newspaper photos.

When the person is doing something familiar, something that we might be doing ourselves, the impact is increased.

People who use your products identify with a photograph of that product. People who work for your company, or live in the community where your company or where one of its affiliates is located, can identify with your company. When your company participates in community activities, especially when you help out in a crisis situation—people identify.

A Good Publicity Picture Has Something to Say

Newspaper and magazine editors call it the storytelling quality. In publicity, it is more likely simply to say something on behalf of your company or what you sell. However, it is always true that the closer the photo comes to reaching into the reader's life or the more the reader can vicariously identify with the person or action in the photograph, the louder and clearer the picture speaks.

A recent newspaper photograph that spoke eloquently was the picture of New York's incumbent mayor and the mayor-elect walking away from a crowd. Their backs were to the camera. The mayor's arm was around the shoulders of the mayor-elect.

Could this picture have said as much if the incumbent mayor had been handing the mayor-elect a gavel? Hardly. Yet we generally settle for the classic hand-off of the gavel. Why? Because it's easy. It's what you see all the time and therefore think it's expected. It's expected all right—but only because that's about all an editor gets. If you want an edge with an editor—use your imagination.

Even the photograph of a building under construction should have something important to say, something like: "This is a growth company." The financial community as well as your customers would like that message.

A Good Publicity Picture Has Emotional Impact

In 1971 Coca-Cola featured a television commercial showing young people from around the world who had gathered on a hillside outside Rome to sing about global harmony. This commercial reached far beyond advertising. It seemed to strike a sympathetic chord in all of us. The results of the publicity could be seen and heard almost everywhere.

Nearly twenty years later Coca-Cola reassembled—on that same hillside—not only the original cast, but their children, as well. They sang a song based on the original. A lot of publicity? You'd better believe it!

It is the rare person who fails to react strongly and emotionally to a great many of the news pictures today—pictures of hurricanes, earthquakes, tornadoes, hunger, homelessness. They have tremendous emotional impact. It's mighty difficult to look at any photograph of a disaster scene without identifying with it: "What if this happened to me? What would I do?"

Posed pictures rarely arouse this sort of emotion, but occasionally a good photographer catches an expression on the face of a child or a pet, on the face of a mother or father interacting with a child, or on the expression of someone in a company concentrating so hard on what he is doing that the observer is drawn right into the picture. At least you always should be alert for just such a picture, and make sure your photographer knows that you are looking for it, too.

Put Action in Your Picture

Action doesn't necessarily require people running around and jumping. Often this just means taking an unposed picture. I found a good example of this in my files. The photo was taken when Mikhail Baryshnikov was signing autographs for shoppers at Saks Fifth Avenue. The caption explained: "The ballet star was making an appearance to promote 'Misha,' a new perfume that bears his nickname."

Now, this doesn't seem like an action shot, does it? Yet there was a lot of action. One woman was holding out a picture to be autographed, a young man was talking to a smiling Mikhail and there was a photographer in the background. Usually, photographing another photographer is a no-no, but in this instance the popping of a flashbulb heightened the sense of action.

The best pictures convey action or a candid view. Of what? People standing in a line staring glassy eyed at the camera? Shaking hands? One person handing a gavel to another person? Cutting a ribbon? A group of people holding a trophy? These are the old standbys. Try to get better pictures by having your subjects doing something interesting.

What about a Diggs "award": all the coins you can shovel in five minutes? Instead of a ribbon cutting, the challenge of digging your way through a mound of ribbons?

Try to Get Beauty into Your Photographs

Industries and businesses rarely lend themselves to beauty, but a good photographer can get what is called a "pattern shot" showing views of inanimate objects arranged in interesting patterns. Also, this beauty can be found in the face of one of your oldest employees—who is concentrating on making a Diggs shovel. Can you find beauty in the expressions on the faces of a child and his grandfather as they work together to shovel snow after a blizzard? What about John Diggs and his grandchild?

Choose Your Background Carefully

In the shovel pictures, the park is the background. It is the only place such a picture can logically be taken. I've had clients who wanted to milk the situation for every ounce of publicity, insisting that the picture be taken at the factory where their product was made. Not John Diggs. He knows that by using the park as a background, he will actually get more positive publicity because everyone in town is interested in a cleaner, more inviting park. No one gives a darn about the Diggs factory.

If your photographs are taken during an event like a banquet or press conference, your background has been chosen for you. Your photographer must get the pictures as they occur. This does not mean, however, that you can't restage the event at a later time to cover yourself.

On the other hand, if you arrange a photo opportunity, check out the place where the pictures are to be taken in advance. Don't be caught by surprise. Make sure that there is at least one plain white or light-colored wall that you can use as a background. In an emergency it's a good idea to have a white dropcloth handy, with, of course, something to tack it up. To keep your background simple, avoid anything that might distract from the subject.

When you are really stuck with something objectionable or distracting behind the subject, your photographer may be able to blur the background sufficiently by opening the lens wide. In an emergency this is worth a try. ,

There are always exceptions. One might be when you want an appropriate background to help identify the person or product. This type of picture might be a picture of the company president at a desk, a factory worker at a machine, or a product in the type of environment where it is used.

IF YOU CAN POSSIBLY AFFORD IT, HIRE A PROFESSIONAL PHOTOGRAPHER

Yes, I know there are cameras today that do all the work for you. If they really do all the work, then why is it that so many pictures are still so incredibly bad?

The fact is, few of us take the time to really understand what makes a good picture. The camera can only record. You are the one who makes sure the photograph is good publicity. A camera can't tell you to get closer to the subject. It can't tell you to find a better background. It can't tell you how to make the picture interesting.

Most publicists make suggestions but find it profitable to heed the photographer's advice.

In some cases these decisions are the responsibility of the photographer, but if it's your company or your product, you'd be foolish to bank on his or her judgment alone.

Finally, advance agreement about costs with the photographer is good budget insurance.

Hiring the Right Photographer for Your Job

For years I used the same photographer for all my clients' publicity photographs. He was good, and he was dependable. So when a friend asked me to recommend a photographer to take pictures of her newly decorated apartment, I recommended him. Mistake. Bad mistake. The pictures were dull, flat, and uninteresting.

This was before I went to work for a decorating magazine. There I learned about the time, lighting, effort, and detail that go into properly photographing a room or even a product. Joe was terrific on news shots. Products and interiors need specialists. There are even important differences and, therefore choices, among specialists.

An interior designer told me that a friend recommended a photographer who specializes in interiors. I suggested that he go through magazines and check out the work before he committed himself. In doing so, he discovered the work of another photographer he liked better.

However they are obtained, your publicity photographs must meet professional standards. There's a lot of competition out there for newspaper and magazine space. An amateurish photograph simply doesn't make it. In addition to the essential professional qualities of the print itself—clear and sharp on glossy paper—your picture should be 8 × 10 or 5 × 7 inches, since square or tall pictures don't fit naturally into a newspaper column.

HOW TO WRITE, TYPE, AFFIX YOUR CAPTION, AND MAIL THE PICTURE

As mentioned earlier, there must always be a caption for every photograph you send out. This caption must clearly identify each person, except professional models, in the picture (from left to right) and explain any action in the photograph. The caption for a new product picture should clearly explain the product's purpose and uses.

Your caption should be typed double-spaced, but the copy (including return address) should begin halfway down the page since the upper half of the 8½ × 11 inch sheet is attached to the back of the picture. (Never write on the back of the photograph.)

With rubber cement, attach the top half of the paper to the back of the photograph, showing the typed copy facing so the editor can see the picture and the copy at the same time. For mailing, fold the typed side (the bottom half) up over the picture.

When mailing or even hand-delivering photographs, protect them from cracking by inserting them in a manila envelope with cardboard of the same size. Especially if you use only one cardboard, point the glossy image side toward the back of the envelope so that the post office stamp doesn't damage the print. Your envelope should be stamped: "Photographs: Do Not Bend."

SAMPLE PICTURE CAPTION

The photograph to which this caption is affixed shows John Diggs making the first "dig" in the park project, teaching a very young volunteer how to use a shovel, giving volunteers shovels of all different sizes.

The Diggs Shovel Company
Address:
Telephone:
Contact:

FOR RELEASE APRIL 1 OR THEREAFTER

JOHN DIGGS IS SHOVELING OFF TO BUFFALO

John Diggs, president of the Diggs Shovel Company, takes a dig at the city park. He is helping to launch a full-scale restoration of the park for the people of this city by donating a truckload of Diggs shovels. Here he shows volunteers the proper method for using a shovel.

CHAPTER PERSPECTIVE

This chapter tackled the problems and possibilities of publicity photographs. This is very important to you in your search for publicity because a good photo can often make the difference between a story that is well received or one that is not printed. Good pictures attract attention—the attention of both the media and its audience. Once you have mastered the material in this chapter, you will find that you have become an expert at analyzing each photograph—before it is too late to change it.

How to Create Your Mailing Lists

INTRODUCTION AND MAIN POINTS

In this chapter we will assist you in preparing mailing lists for all your publicity needs: local, regional, national and international. We will give you in even greater detail information about all the media: newspapers, consumer magazines, business-to-business publications, television, radio, and the wire services. This is the further information you will need before compiling and finalizing your mailing lists. In this chapter you will be given the names and addresses of media directories so you will be able to compile the media lists best suited to your specific needs.

After studying the material in this chapter:

■ You will learn the difference between horizontal and vertical media.

■ You will understand the necessity of keeping separate lists for each type of media.

■ You will find out how to determine the types of lists you may need.

■ You will learn how to obtain the names of special-interest editors most likely to use your publicity.

■ You will begin to understand when it is time for your publicity to branch out geographically.

■ You will learn how to prepare local, regional, national, and international publicity mailing lists.

All right now, you've learned to write a news release and you've learned to take good news photos, but if you don't know what to do with them, they won't do you or your business a lick of good—a bit like getting all dressed up with no place to go.

So what do you do? It's time for you to prepare your mailing lists. Yes, I said lists—more than one—in fact, several, maybe many. But mailings cost money—sometimes lots of money, so plan your lists with discretion. If you believe that one newspaper can give you enough publicity for your purposes, concentrate on the needs and requirements of that newspaper. When contemplating large regional or national mailings, remember that you can use all or a select few. There is no rule, and your only true guideline is your company, product, or service publicity needs and your sales needs.

LEARN THE DIFFERENCE BETWEEN HORIZONTAL AND VERTICAL MEDIA

We must clarify first that there are two different types of mailing lists.

Horizontal mailing lists deal with mass media and have the cross section of the public as its audience. This type of mailing list is valuable to you only if your message or your product is of universal interest—if all types of people, all ages, are potential buyers.

Vertical mailing lists target the audience to special interests. These special interests may vary from sports to art to very specialized business-to-business publicity. This type of medium focuses on a specific interest group. Even if yours is a universally interesting product or service, you may have messages that are for a specific interest group.

KEEP SEPARATE LISTS FOR EACH TYPE OF MEDIUM

You'll find that there are occasions when you want to make a mailing to a specific type of medium—large metropolitan dailies, smaller daily papers, weekly newspapers, television, or radio. It's a good idea to begin by keeping them in separate lists so they can be easily extracted for a particular use. Also, it is easier to expand these lists as your geographic areas become larger.

Other lists you want to keep separate include consumer magazines, wire services, syndicated services, special-interest publications, and business-to-business publications, such as trade, professional, and technical journals.

TYPES OF LISTS YOU MAY NEED

You may need only one or two lists of a very limited nature to begin with, but it pays to plan for future lists at this time as well. The reason for this is to establish a workable pattern for your lists: how you keep them, the type of information you collect, that sort of thing. As you prepare more and more lists, you can shuffle and combine them for temporary or immediate goals. This eliminates the need to build a new list each time you send out a mailing. The lists you may eventually be building include:

- Company "hometown" media
- Branch office "hometown" media
- Wire services
- Daily newspapers (A list: 100,000 circulation or more)
- Daily newspapers (B list: 50,000–100,000 circulation)
- Weekly newspapers (C list)
- Syndicated columnists
- Television stations
- Radio stations
- Trade, professional, and technical journals
- Consumer publications
- Media in countries throughout the world

FIRST, PREPARE A LOCAL PUBLICITY MAILING LIST

Your community may be a small town or a large metropolitan city, but it's your town: it's home. Companies, like people, like to be well known and well liked in their own communities. They like to be good neighbors.

When you get involved in community events, you probably want to send out a press release to the community media. When you hold a special event in your home offices, you want to notify the community. But you will be far too busy getting ready, as well as carrying on business, to decide at the last moment to whom you send a news release. Do it now.

Compiling your local list may be as simple as consulting the classified section of your local telephone book. You also should attempt to obtain as many lists as possible from such sources as trade associations, advertising agencies, the chamber of commerce, other companies and corporations, and any other organization with which you might have a connection.

Your Local Mailing List Should Include the Mass Media

The need to obtain the names and addresses of all the local newspapers, television, and radio stations is obvious. What may not be so obvious as avenues of local publicity are the ethnic newspapers and perhaps even those "throwaway" newspapers you find at your front door. Also, some communities have small magazines. Don't forget these.

List Names of Editors and Other Personal Contacts

You want the name of the editor if yours is a small town, neighborhood, or suburban weekly or the name of the city editor if yours is a larger daily newspaper. Make very sure that the name is spelled correctly. Remember, check your list for changes each time you use it. When you send general news items to television and radio stations, ask for the name of the news editor.

These guidelines vary only if you have a very good contact who can give your publicity release an added push. Just one note of caution, however: don't overdo a good thing. If you know someone who will do you a good turn, save the favor for something important.

Get the Name of Each Special-Interest Editor or Columnist

There may be many special-interest editors and columnists on your local newspapers or talk show hosts and producers at the television and radio stations. As you go through your newspaper, list each one as well as every special section—sports, society, arts, leisure, home improvement, and food—you get the idea. The one special-interest editor you definitely want is the business editor.

The special section editors and columnists you want on your mailing list depend on your type of business as well as on your product or service. For instance, if you sell a sports item, you obviously want the name of the sports editor, but it's not likely you have any use for the name of the home improvement editor. Of course, you send these editors product or service news only when it is of special interest to their particular readers.

If the name of the editor you're interested in isn't listed, call and find out who is.

WHEN IT'S TIME FOR YOUR PUBLICITY TO BRANCH OUT GEOGRAPHICALLY

Your local mailing list, and the way you have prepared it, should be the pattern for preparing all other lists you may want or need. The only major difference is that instead of making telephone calls to check names and addresses, you use media directories. Some are single directories, and some come in sets, each book concentrating on a geographic area or a specific type of medium.

You should be able to find these media directories in your local library, usually in the general reference section. You won't be able to take them out, however, so be sure to take a stack of file cards (3 × 5, 4 × 6, or 5 × 8 inch) and pens or pencils with you. If you want to buy a media directory, you will find a list of their names and addresses, plus a short description of their contents and specialities, at the end of this chapter.

Your Company May Have More Than One "Hometown"

If yours is a large company with several branch offices, distribution centers, or retail stores, each should have its own "hometown" mailing list for times when you want to release news affecting only that particular branch, community, or region.

Prepare a List for Each of Your Sales Distribution Areas

In many instances, your business news may affect only a specific sales distribution area. A mailing list for this area can often solve immediate problems in the shortest possible time. Also, this type of list is particularly advantageous if you want to test market or introduce a new product into a single region before taking the product to national distribution.

Prepare a Mailing List for Regional Publicity

The most practical regional publicity list for you includes your sales distribution area or areas. This might include several states, or portions of several states, depending upon the location of both your customers and potential customers.

It might include every city and town in your state or perhaps only a particular type of town or city in the state. For instance, if yours is a farm product and your sales distribution area is in only one state, your mailing list may include only the farm community media within that state. On the other hand, if your product is one sold only in metropolitan areas—well, you get the idea.

You don't have to be a national company for a national mailing list to be of value. There are several reasons you might need a national mailing list. You might want to improve the image of your company, product, or service. You might want to test the waters before "going national." Even a local event can take on national proportions when it has the potential to affect enough people.

You want separate lists for large and small daily newspapers, weekly newspapers, television stations, radio stations, trade, professional, and technical journals, consumer publications, wire services, syndicated services and columnists, and publications interested in your own special interests.

INFORMATION YOU WANT TO RECORD

Once you have the name of the publication (or other medium) you are aiming for, you want to obtain the following information and keep it on the index card. Make up a card for each publication, television, or radio show.
- Name of publication or show
- Address
- Telephone number
- Date and frequency of publication
- Publisher's name
- Editor's name
- Name of any other key personnel for publicity purposes
- Deadline date and time
- Field covered
- Circulation coverage
- Classification (mass media, architecture, medicine, association, institutional, age group, and so on)

KEEP YOUR LISTS WHERE YOU CAN GET TO THEM EASILY AND QUICKLY

Today, with computers, making lists and keeping them up-to-date isn't quite the job it used to be, but it's still a considerable amount of work. Just remember, it's worth it. If you don't have electronic equipment or simply don't want to use it for mailing lists, try using index cards (3 × 5, 4 × 6, or 5 × 8 inch cards, depending upon the amount of information you need). Be sure to have one card for each name and address.

Separate the cards into whatever categories work best for you. You may find that you draw from several categories for special mailings, and once used, be sure each card gets "home" so you can find it the next time.

CHECK YOUR LIST FOR CHANGES EACH TIME YOU USE IT

Just as in any other profession, editors move on to other things and new editors take their place. Check that your list is up-to-date before consigning even the smallest or most insignificant story to it. Sending a story or photograph to an editor who is no longer there doesn't earn you any brownie points with the current editor.

WHEN YOU NEED A PROFESSIONAL SERVICE TO SEND OUT YOUR RELEASE

There may come a time when you need an outside agency to take the load of mailing off your shoulders, or you may find it expedient to retain an outside agency to handle all your mailings. When you want or need a specialized mailing firm to help you, there are local and national organizations from which you can choose. Keep in mind that there are many differences in the way they work and the areas they cover, so do your homework before you spend a lot of money. For instance, some may supply you with master lists from which you type the labels. Others send you the labels already typed, and all you have to do is attach them to your envelopes. The full service companies handle everything from reproducing your press release to sending it to any list you specify. Make very sure you know in advance precisely what to expect and how much it costs, including postage. You may be able to find the perfect mailing service in your own community, but one of the biggest and best national services is

BACON'S PR AND MEDIA INFORMATION SYSTEMS
332 South Michigan Avenue
Chicago IL 60604

You can call (800)621-0561 for a brochure outlining their services and costs. You also can buy Bacon's media directories.

YOU CAN COMPILE YOUR MAILING LISTS FROM MEDIA DIRECTORIES

Media directories are just that: books filled with the names, addresses, telephone numbers, and all other pertinent information you need. Some of them specialize in the print media, some in television and radio, and others cover the entire gamut of the media. Most of them are broken down by geographic areas. In most of these volumes you find all the contacts you need, plus addresses, telephone numbers, and, in many instances, a description of the information they are interested in receiving.

Plan to spend plenty of time at your local library to go through all the available media directories and find those that are best for your purposes. If you don't have the time to spend at the library and can afford it, these media directories can be purchased. Call or write for a complete description of the directories, and ask for current prices.

PLAN IN ADVANCE THE LISTS YOU NEED

Because media directories cover such a vast number of media, it helps if you have determined your immediate needs even before you go to the library. Ask yourself these questions:

▬ In which cities or regions do I need publicity right now?
▬ Should I concentrate on weeklies, midsize dailies, or large metropolitan newspapers?
▬ On which business-to-business publications should I concentrate first?
▬ Do I need television and radio lists at this time?

These are just sample questions, of course. You have your own special needs and questions that should be answered even before you go to the library. Once there, the librarian can help you find the best media directories for your needs.

THE MAJOR MEDIA DIRECTORIES

WORKING PRESS OF THE NATION   (800)456-4555
National Research Bureau
424 North Third Street
Burlington, IA 52601

This media directory comes in five separate volumes: newspapers, magazines, television and radio stations, feature writers and photographers, and internal publications. Here you find daily, weekly, and special-interest newspapers, syndicates, news bureaus, photo and wire services, consumer and trade publications, and broadcast stations.

THE EDITOR & PUBLISHER   (212)675-4380
   YEAR BOOK
11 West 19th Street
New York, NY 10011

This is a directory of all the daily and nondaily newspapers in the United States, including those serving college, trade, foreign language, black, professional, or other specialized audiences. You also find a list of news services, feature syndicates, and magazine sections, and a list of newspapers published in foreign countries.

EDITOR & PUBLISHER SYNDICATE   (212)675-4380
   DIRECTORY
11 West 19th Street
New York, NY 10011

This directory is a source of news and feature syndicates throughout the United States. It also describes the type of information covered by different syndicated columns.

BROADCASTING/CABLE YEAR   (800)638-7827
   BOOK
1705 DeSales St. N.W.
Washington, DC 20036-4480

As the title suggests, this directory gives you the names, titles, and phone numbers of key contacts for every commercial and noncommercial television and radio station in the United States and Canada. It provides formats of the stations, plus the hours per week of news, special, or foreign language programming.

IF YOUR BUSINESS IS GLOBAL, YOU WANT A GLOBAL DIRECTORY

One of the best media directories for companies with international interests is

Benn Business Information
  Services Ltd.   0732 362666
P.O. Box 20 Sovereign Way   Telex: 95454 BBIS G
Tonbridge Kent TN9 1RQ   Fax: 0732 770483
England

This is a two-volume guide to the world's media. The international volume lists media in 197 countries, covering the world's press, broadcasting, and communications services. The companion volume gives details on media in the United Kingdom.

CHAPTER PERSPECTIVE

This chapter expanded the discussion of the media in an effort to help you build your mailing lists long before you need them. When you make decisions about the type of mailing list you need at any given moment, you can find here the methods for selecting the most appropriate media in the targeted geographic areas. The importance of keeping your mailing lists flexible and, especially, up to date was emphasized.

What You Should Know about the Consumer Print Media

INTRODUCTION AND MAIN POINTS

In this chapter we will help you understand the consumer print media: newspapers, consumer magazines, and wire services. We also will explain how and why each publication attracts a different audience, and how the wire services effectively service all publications. We will guide you in studying each of these media so you will be better able to plan your publicity to fit their needs. In this chapter we also deal with the timing of your news releases for the greatest possible print coverage.

After studying the material in this chapter:

■ You will understand how you can best utilize the print media to get publicity for your company, products, and services.

■ You will learn about the three categories of newspapers and the needs of each category.

■ You will learn how wire services operate and how you can best utilize their services.

■ You will learn about consumer magazines and their needs.

■ You will learn about the importance of meeting media deadlines and of timing your releases to do so.

On a crowded city bus recently a young mother was loudly reading a story about a honey bear to a very young child. Also on that bus were people of all ages, ethnic backgrounds, and job descriptions. Many of them were obviously annoyed.

Most of these adults had probably read such stories to their own children, so why were they upset? When you think about it, those riders were justifiably annoyed. That children's story would have been a big hit in a kindergarten class, but in that setting and at that time it was inappropriate for that audience.

Each consumer publication has its own special-interest "riders." It is the editor's job to keep those rider-readers comfortable and content. For instance, a responsible editor doesn't publish a children's story in a sports magazine.

Therefore, before you send a press release to a consumer magazine, think like the editor of that consumer magazine and consider whether your news is of interest to his or her readers. If not, keep looking until you find the consumer publication in which your press release is appropriate—the media "bus" that carries your type of "rider."

MOST NEWSPAPERS ARE INTERESTED IN STORIES WITH UNIVERSAL APPEAL

Have you ever clipped a recipe from a newspaper? What about an article on home repair? If you sell a food item or a home repair product, newspapers are the perfect medium to publicize your product. Most of us like to keep our homes in good repair, and all of us—despite our special and unique interests—must eat; therefore, anything about these two subjects generally catches our attention. These products are of interest to the masses, and therefore to the mass media.

With the right newsworthy approach the Diggs shovel is a natural for the mass media. It's a product everyone uses at least once in his or her lifetime. Diggs sets up shovel teams to help the elderly and handicapped dig out after a snow storm: if they do it in Dayton, it's a local Dayton story. If they do it all across the country, or if John Diggs says he's looking for volunteers throughout the country, this is a potential wire service story.

In publicity, as in so many other things, there is a place for everything and everything should be in its proper place. For example, would you even glance at a newspaper article about a new machine for the lumber industry? It is up to you to decide upon the best place for your publicity. To make this determination, you should know as much as possible about the media you are considering.

NEWSPAPERS ARE DIVIDED INTO THREE CATEGORIES

There are nearly 10,000 newspapers in the United States alone. Of these more than 1700 are daily newspapers, and well over 7500 are weekly papers.

Obviously, you're not about to get a publicity story into all these papers, but consider the vast opportunities available to your company, product, and service.

For convenient reference, newspapers in America are generally divided into three categories: the A, B, and C groups. Before you can even hope to break into print, you should know something about these publications.

The A group includes the large metropolitan dailies with a circulation of 100,000 or more. The B group are those daily newspapers with circulations of 50,000 to 100,000. The C group includes the weekly newspapers.

TRY TO GET YOUR HANDS ON EACH TYPE OF NEWSPAPER

It will be difficult for you to understand the needs of a publication you have never seen. For this reason, it is imperative that you study at least one example of each category of newspaper before you blindly send out publicity stories.

As previously stated, there are well over 1700 daily newspapers and 7500 weekly newspapers in the United States alone. Even if you live in a very small town, your library probably carries at least one newspaper of each category, probably those published in your own state. If you can locate others, so much the better, as the more papers you can examine, you can better understand the needs and demands of the media.

BEFORE TRYING TO GET NEWSPAPER PUBLICITY, DO YOUR HOMEWORK

Take the time to read carefully through each of the newspapers. Note the sort of stories they carry. Pay particular attention to articles about other companies, products, or services. Try to figure out why a particular story was accepted by a specific newspaper. Is it a news story? Is it a feature or human interest story? Is there an accompanying photograph? Is it in the news section or one of the special-interest sections? If it is a special-interest section, which one, and why? Don't just do your research. Try to understand the why of it as well.

The most important thing to keep in mind is that all newspapers, despite vast differences in circulation, have one thing in common. They are edited for readers who have a broad spectrum of interests. Thus, newspapers are often referred to as the "horizontal media."

The small town where I grew up had a weekly newspaper. Each week my mother would get a telephone call from the editor asking if she had any news to report—guests, trips, parties, special occasions, that sort of thing. Local news about local people was the backbone of that newspaper.

Weekly newspapers are found not only in small towns, but also in the suburbs of large cities. Newspapers that serve a particular region or ethnic group are also typically published weekly.

These newspapers are generally more interested in you and your relationship with their locale and/or special interests than they are in your company, your product, or your service. It is because of these newspapers that you want to know the hometowns of every employee in your company, so when someone does something special—wins an award, comes up with a new product idea, or even gets married—you have a ready-made audience for a publicity mention of your company.

Daily Papers in Midsize Cities Want Local and National News

During my college days, I was a reporter for a daily newspaper in a midsized city. Local news was covered by reporters as thoroughly as possible. In addition, when a national story with a local angle came over the wires, a reporter would be dispatched to get more information to write the story from a local point of view.

I can't imagine the editor calling anyone at home asking for family news, but we treated with great respect any news about local people, whether it came from someone making a telephone call to the editor, a wire service story with a local angle, or even a publicity release involving a hometown person.

It is this local angle about your business that gets the best coverage in these smaller dailies. When you send out a news release about your company, product, or service, you have a far greater chance of being published in any paper when you include a local angle: when you promote someone formerly from this community or when a "local" is responsible for a new product or service. Also, there may be some connection with a local company—a dealer or manufacturer. Or something about your company, product, or service could affect the lives of local people, local business, or the community in general.

Some Large Metropolitan Dailies Must Appeal to Millions

Today *The New York Times* is delivered to my door each morning. I am only one of its 1,680,217 daily readers, yet there is always something in it that interests each of us. How can one newspaper possibly appeal to nearly two million readers with such a variety of interests?

Simple: there is something in *The New York Times* for everybody. If you can get a copy of this newspaper, you will discover that not only does it cover local, regional, national, and international news, but it also has special editors and even entire sections dedicated to business, food, home furnishings, sports, gardens, education, arts, aviation, books, theater, music, news, television and radio, real estate, religion, science, society, and travel—and new products. On Sunday, the *Times* also has special magazine sections.

If you have an article about a new product or service, be sure to send it to the appropriate editor of any suitable publication.

Among the dailies, there are both morning and afternoon newspapers. Among the thousands of large circulation newspapers, by far the largest number are published in the afternoon (the PMs); however, some of the most influential and powerful newspapers are published in the morning (the AMs). There are a handful—thirtysomething—with editions that come out all day long. These are called "all-day" papers.

The Wire Services Cover All These Things

How does any one newspaper, regardless of size, obtain access to stories from all over the world? In the case of *The New York Times* you often find the phrase: "Special to *The New York Times*." In most instances, though, news comes from one or more of the wire services. This does not mean that news is actually transmitted over the telegraph wire, but the term originates from those times when it was. Today wire service news is more likely to be transmitted via satellite.

You can't think "news" without thinking wire services. Although no wire service publishes a newspaper, they provide most of the media with the news that is published. They are central to all news reporting. If you have a good and timely news story about your company, product, or service, it's a good idea to check with one of these news services to see if they will put it over the wires. If they're interested, you're really in luck.

Editors all over the world check the wires day in and day out, pulling those stories of interest to their specific audiences. Some stories are used verbatim. Some are used as starters, with editors sending out their own reporters to flesh out the wire service story or to give their readers a fresh or local angle.

THE FOUR MAJOR WIRE SERVICES

The wire services you hear most about are the AP (Associated Press), UPI (United Press International), Dow Jones, and Reuters. All of them are international. AP, UPI, and Dow Jones are dominant in America. Reuters is a British news agency that, although strongest abroad and in international financial reporting, is expanding its operations in the United States.

The wire services serve thousands of newspapers throughout the world with news and photographs at all levels: local, state, national, and international. Their purpose is to provide every editor with every sort of story and every bit of information needed to publish a paper every single day.

The AP, a nonprofit business organized as a cooperative, is owned by the media it serves. The largest and the oldest of the wire services, it has about 120 U.S. bureaus that provide the news to more than 1300 daily newspapers in the United States alone. When I called AP to find out how many there are around the world, the man to whom I was speaking just laughed. There are a lot of them.

UPI is a privately owned company and reports that it has more than 1000 clients.

The Dow Jones News Service, or "Broadtape," is the cooperative effort of journalists from Dow Jones and *The Wall Street Journal.* Its companion service, the Dow Jones International News Service, has correspondents stationed in key financial and business centers around the world, as well as the news-gathering resources of the Associated Press and Dow-Jones.

The British news service Reuters is known primarily as an international agency, especially in the reporting of international financial news.

No matter where you live or have your business, you can bet that there is a press service bureau or "stringer" nearby. If your community does not have a wire service bureau and bureau chief, it is probable that someone at the local newspaper is a designated "stringer," or on-the-spot representative. Call and find out. If you can interest a bureau or stringer in a story or photograph, you have the opportunity to reach media all over the world.

How can you study the wire services when they don't publish anything themselves? Check the dateline in every newspaper you can get your hands on. If it says something like "Palm Springs, Calif., May 3 (AP)," this is obviously a story picked up from the wires. Study it. Clip each one you can find. You'll probably discover that most of them lead in to stories of national or international importance: politics, disasters, big business deals—that sort of thing. Perhaps this is not in your league; certainly it won't be very often, but once in a while you'll run across a "human interest" story or photograph that media all over the country or perhaps all over the world run simply because it is so unusual, so interesting, so warming, or so humorous. Cherish these. Refer to them often. I don't mean that you should imitate them. No! But learn from them. Once you find enough of them, you sense a pattern. You begin to see what the editors see. And you are better able to judge your own stories and photographs in the light of what is most likely of interest to editors. In other words, you are better able to give them what they want.

TIMING YOUR RELEASE IS IMPORTANT

As a general rule, afternoon newspapers (PMs) usually go to press from 11 a.m. to 3 p.m. If your press release is being delivered, be sure it gets there no later than 9 a.m.

The morning papers usually go to press between 6 p.m. and 11 p.m. Deliver your story no later than noon the day before.

There also are special considerations: the Sunday and Monday newspapers are traditionally the best days for publicity since more space is available in the Sunday paper and there is less news to report on a Monday. Try to avoid days when local or even national events are likely to take over all the available space, leaving your publicity in the cold.

Weekly newspapers are usually issued on a Wednesday or Thursday, which means their deadlines are probably two days before that.

Always check with the newspaper for information about their specific deadlines and other requirements.

CONSUMER MAGAZINES LEAN TOWARD SPECIAL INTERESTS

What does *Time Magazine* have in common with *Vogue* and *Popular Mechanix*? They are classified as consumer publications, but that's about all they have in common. One person might read all three but for very different reasons. Today, most consumer magazines are special-interest or "vertical" publications.

Over the past few years, magazines have changed a great deal simply because the reading public has changed. In the past, the professional technician had to read a professional journal to get the facts and details needed. Today, because amateur "buffs" are so well informed, a new type of special-interest publication—a "hybrid" medium—has become popular.

You are probably already familiar with the consumer magazines that cater to your type of product or service. You should study them carefully, however, to see how you can fit the news from your company into their format. If you have a new product, you may discover that the new products column is your best bet. Maybe there is an opportunity for general news items. Only studying the publications will tell you.

Also, because of technical advances in the publishing field, a very recent development among magazines is the trend to regional editions. At this time only a few publications have gone beyond regional advertising into regional editorial coverage, but watch for developments in this area that might affect your opportunities for publicity.

In dealing with magazines, it is a good idea to send what is known as a "query" letter to the editor instead of sending a news release. In this letter to the editor, explain why you believe your story is of interest to the magazine's readers and back it up by sending any available supporting material: news release, photographs, and, if practical, even a sample of the product.

GIVE THE EDITORS WHAT THEIR READERS WANT

It's an interesting thing about editors, whether of a newspaper, wire service, or magazine: when you give them a story that is sure to please their readers, they are warm, generous, and affable people. When you send them something off the mark, they can be brusk and intimidating.

The moral of this story: send an editor only those stories you know are right for his or her publication. Don't waste their time. This requires that you take the time and effort to study each publication. You'll find it's worth it.

CHAPTER PERSPECTIVE

This chapter discussed how you can focus your news and publicity needs so that they meet the requirements of the various categories of newspapers, consumer magazines, and wire services or news agencies. It stressed the importance of studying the examples before you every day. This chapter sought to impress upon you the necessity of doing your homework, using the best textbooks in the world: the media themselves.

Getting Publicity on Television and Radio

INTRODUCTION AND MAIN POINTS

In this chapter we will give you a glimpse of television and radio from the inside. Once you understand some of the problems faced by reporters, commentators, assignment editors, and producers each day, you can give them what they want and what they need to serve the public. We try to show how the act of getting publicity is more a matter of providing assistance to the media than simply prodding the press for free time.

After studying the material in this chapter:

▬ You will be able to identify the news in your company and present it so that it gets the maximum publicity.

▬ You will understand what talk shows look for in guests and how to give this to them.

▬ You will learn how to compete for an assignment editor's attention.

▬ You will get tips on how to schedule important events for the best publicity results.

▬ You will be informed of the newest and best in publicity vehicles.

You think it's tough getting on television? Don't be silly. It's a snap. Just watch all those "Hi Mom!" wavers behind the reporter during a live remote. Those people are on television. If all you want is to get on television, all you really have to do is follow a TV camera crew around town—and wave.

However, if you want to be on television to get publicity for your business, then you must learn the most productive methods of making yourself, your products, your services, and your company of interest to television editors and interviewers.

TELEVISION AND RADIO NEED YOU AS MUCH AS YOU NEED THEM

Has is ever occurred to you just how important you are to the media? There is no news unless people like you make it. There is no business news unless people like you create it.

All too often we think we have to please the media. This, quite simply, is just not true. All we have to do is create news of interest to other people just like ourselves. It is the sole function of the media to report the news. It's not their fault if the news we give them isn't as interesting or as important as the news someone else gives them. It isn't their fault if we report what news we have in such a way that it doesn't come across as important. It isn't their fault if we don't report it at all.

Why the Same Business People Are Interviewed Again and Again

Does the names Lee Iacocca a bell? It should. He was the favorite spokesperson for the auto industry throughout the 1980s. Why was he so much in demand? In other words, what does a television reporter look for in an interview? Here are a few guidelines:

▬ Reporters tend to seek out business people who are acknowledged leaders in their fields and often seek comments from business persons with familiar names.

▬ Reporters prefer to go to a reliable source. Frequently, the fastest and easiest thing to do is contact authoritative business people who have been quoted before.

▬ Business people who keep themselves well briefed and up-to-date—especially in their particular field—and who are prepared at a moment's notice to provide educated remarks are at a premium. This is important because reporters don't have time to waste when they are working against a tight deadline.

▬ Reporters are looking for someone who can discuss the subject in plain, easy-to-understand English and who can explain it in an orderly way.

▬ The media likes "pithy" comments (quotable quotes). The business person who is good at "punditry" is more likely to be interviewed on television.

■ Sometimes reporters want to interview business people with extreme opinions. This is usually a plus when an interviewer wants a point-counterpoint discussion.

■ Finally, a reporter may call simply because a particular business person is in his file or once returned a phone call.

TELEVISION AND RADIO ARE ALWAYS LOOKING FOR INTERESTING PEOPLE

There are two types of programs that offer the best possible forum for business people just like you: news shows and interview shows. Audience participation shows may boost your ego but they can do little to help you sell your product or increase your business. One reason is that they are not geared to give your business publicity. Another reason is that they give you no opportunity to display your professional or business expertise.

So, how can you get on a television or radio news or talk show? Do your homework. Watch and listen to every news and talk show you possibly can with the sole purpose of understanding their format. Try to figure out how you can fit your product, your service, and your business into that format. See how others do it. Don't just imitate—plan ways to do it better.

Give Them Something They Can't Refuse: News

Whether it's a news show or a talk show, you have an edge if you can produce a news angle to your story. In other words, why call them now? Why not last week or next week?

Because, of course, you want the publicity right now. Unless you have uncanny influence or news is mighty scarce that particular day, this reason won't sell anyone in the media to grant your wishes.

A good news story will. This news can be anything from a well-executed media event to the introduction of a new product. Whatever, the news element must be there if you want results.

Learn to Think Like an Assignment Editor

Assignment editors have a tough job. Each day they have to come up with enough news and features to fill hours of television or radio time. They must keep on top of the news, and they can never allow the competition to get ahead of them. To do this, they need all the help they can get.

There are many ways for the media to find out what is going on out there in peopleland. As we discussed previously, they depend a great deal on the wire services (news agencies), which are on duty twenty-four hours a day bringing in news and features from all over the world. They check the competition—all the other media—and they monitor police and fire department radio channels.

They also rely on people who call in to report a news happening. Of course they hope that this news is something dramatic, something really flashy that gets the city or even the world talking. You know the sort of news I'm talking about. In addition, though, there is a lot of other less sensational news out there that they have to report: business news, for example.

Who do they depend on to report the business news? Business people: you. Generally they learn about business news through a well-written news release or perhaps even a telephone call.

You Are Competing for the Assignment Editor's Attention

Despite the fact that there may be hundreds of good news stories, perhaps even a lot of good business news stories, that should or could be covered for a news show, the assignment editor, with a limited number of reporters and/or camera crews, is continually faced with decisions: Which story should we cover? Which story is the most important to our audience? Which story will give our viewers and listeners a little chuckle? Which story is a little offbeat?

Imagine yourself as the assignment editor. Which "tipsters" do you cultivate? Those trying to get on a show just for the sake of publicity, or someone who comes up with a news or feature idea that fills the basic needs of a good news or talk show? Not even a toss-up: You know the answer.

Make It News

There is no reason that publicity should be drab and uninteresting. With a modicum of creative thinking, you should be able to create news for your business.

If you introduce a new product—this is news. If you hold a news conference to announce an important business venture or activity—news again. If you plan a special event—this is news. If you participate in a newsworthy community activity—news. If you tie in with someone already in the news you create an aura of news around yourself and your company. If you do something special before or during a holiday, a major sports event, or a new season, this gives your publicity an element of news.

Look for the Local Angle

Watch the national and international news carefully, and if you can see how your own products or business relates even remotely to the news that day, contact the media and suggest the tie-in. Don't do this casually, though. Don't get a reputation for making an inconsequential pitch at the slightest provocation. Make solid news judgments, both for the sake of your media contacts and for your own business integrity.

The trick is to be extremely well informed about your own industry. You might give a local angle to a national story by commenting on the news as it affects or relates to your business or industry. If there is a big news story on the national or regional television and radio and your business is even remotely related, call the local television and radio stations with a suggested interview topic.

Watch for News that Can Affect the Lives of People Around You

Imagine a big national computer company is in trouble. It is laying off thousands of people. You own a computer store in a mid-size city. You sell the computers this company makes. Many of your customers probably wonder how this crisis affects them: Will they be able to get their computers serviced? Will their equipment become obsolete? Will they be able to expand their equipment?

Only you can find out and give them straight answers. Only you can explain the situation to them in terms they can understand. Only you can relieve the pressures caused by confusion and concern.

What you might do is clip the article you have read in the newspaper, or perhaps in your trade publication, get a sufficient number of photostats to cover all the local broadcast media, and add a personal, typewritten note explaining what this means to their viewers and/or listeners. If the situation calls for action, you might be able to suggest responsible action to be taken.

Become a Guest Expert in Your Field

All the media continually look for guest experts to comment on the news. They particularly seek individuals who can express their views intelligently, understandably, simply, and briefly. The broadcast media also constantly seek the local angle to a national story.

With some effort you can become your local, perhaps eventually even regional or national, guest expert. You see these guest experts all the time, and sometimes, you see the same people over and over again. Why? Because they speak with authority and knowledge and the media need them to interpret the news in their specific fields.

Whether you sell greeting cards, electronics equipment, or farm machinery, stories always pop up in the news, stories that can and even should be explained in local or regional terms. Stories about business can be cold and uninteresting, even though they may affect many people. You can learn to interpret the news in your own field. You have access to all the trade publications in your field. The rest of us don't. You know the intricacies of your business because you work in it day in and day out. The rest of us don't. The fact is, you are an expert in your field. The rest of us are not, but we need to know more about what affects our lives. This is where you come in: explaining the news in your trade, industry, or profession in lay terms, and giving expert opinions on local, regional, national, and international news. You can make yourself into an important guest.

Become thoroughly versed in your industry's news and how it affects the local and national economy. Think these things through in advance, and have your thoughtful opinions ready when needed. Perhaps the business story isn't even reported in your local media but you read about it in trade journals. You see the significance of it and the repercussions in your community or state. Report this.

Once you have proved to the media that you truly understand the problems in your field and that you really are an unbiased expert, you can probably look forward to hearing from the media whenever they want a comment on a subject in your field. In your community, at least, you may become the spokesperson for an industry.

HOW A GUEST EXPERT "SELLS" A COMPANY, PRODUCT OR SERVICE

True, about the only "commercial plug" you get is the mention of your company and your position with the company. Can it improve sales? If you had the choice of buying an expensive product from a company selected by the media to represent the field or from a company down the street that merely touted its own business, which would you trust the most? From which company would you be likely to buy the product? This is called building an image.

Arrange for a Panel of Experts to Comment on the News

If people in your company are highly respected in their own fields—engineering, construction, electronics, and so forth—advise the media of this. Send the news editors a list of your available "experts," along with their biographies and other credentials.

Don't Just Say It—Do It

Television is at its best when it records someone doing something—action. Whenever you can, do something interesting—don't just talk about it. The job of television and radio is to record action, not create it.

You may or may not approve of the way television news has veered into the entertainment area, but this is a fact of life. Whenever it is important for you to get publicity on television or radio, remember that the producers and editors require a dramatic presentation. If they want to keep viewers and listeners tuned in to their shows, they must provide entertainment—action, pathos, violence, sex, confrontation, and controversy—as well as news.

If you want to see just how fast the news media gets to your company to cover the news, give them one or more of these: a company crisis for instance.

Schedule Important Events Early in the Day

If you want a story on the evening news, give the reporters time to get the story and get back to the station to edit their film, write the story, and convince the producer that it will add interest to the show. This is a good general rule, but check with the local stations and find out the best times for them.

Try for an Interesting Live Remote

The live remote is a powerful news coverage tool. It is also a powerful publicity tool.

It's possible that you have lived with live remotes for so long that you hardly notice them anymore. They are those portions of the show when, after a brief lead-in, the anchor says something like, "Now we switch you to Peter Pond in Poughkeepsie." One reason producers like the live remote is that it gives the show a change of pace. The viewer doesn't have to sit through thirty minutes to an hour of one or two people who sit at a desk reading the news.

New technology—continually improved minicams, videotape, and even tape-editing machines—allows reporters to give their viewers on-the-scene coverage of important news events. There isn't an important news story every single day. What are they going to do with this wonderful technology? Let it sit around the studio until something truly worthwhile comes up? Certainly not. Why should they? This would be a waste.

By using your imagination, you can come up with a news event worthy of a live remote. Ask yourself, Is there something really newsworthy going on in my company? Can I turn an announcement into a news event? Can I plan something using our product or service in a dramatic way? Plan special events—media events—around your product, your service, and your company.

Don't place yourself in the position of asking favors of the media. If you can arrange your special event so that viewers really want to know about it then the media will cover it. Remember, viewers and listeners must care before you can make the media care. If you are handicapped or a senior citizen, or have a loved one who is, would you be interested if you saw a troop of Diggs shovelers clearing the sidewalks for others like yourself after a big snowstorm? This is good news to you, but it is also very good publicity for the Diggs Shovel Company.

Ideally, from a news standpoint, live remotes spring up and are covered immediately. When it comes to publicity, however, many editors schedule them in advance. Obviously, if something of greater news interest comes up, your publicity shot may have to be postponed or even canceled. In all likelihood, however, it will be used somewhere, sometime. At least give it a try.

Master the Art of the One-liner

Even the best news story usually runs less than two minutes. A live remote or interview must fit between the introduction and the windup.

I hate to tell you this since it seems a bit of a comedown, but when you are interviewed for a news story, you are called a "sound byte," an interview that usually runs less than forty seconds. Don't take it personally. Even an interview with the mayor is called a sound byte. The sound byte is simply a part of a news package, the filling usually sandwiched between the narration you listen to while you look at pictures and the closer view from the scene by a "stand-upper."

Pay particular attention to interviews with people involved in a story. In addition to being short, their statements are usually very poignant, informative, or dramatic. More important, they help explain the action.

If you can learn the art of making interesting and intriguing sound bytes, statements filled with information or entertainment value, you have a far better chance of seeing yourself on television or hearing your words on radio.

Check the news shows. Time the interviews. Make a note of what is said and how it is said. Of course, the actual interview runs much longer, but all but a brief sound byte is edited out. Give the reporter at least one quotable sound byte so you won't be edited out of the program entirely.

Also, keep in mind that the best speech in the world is usually edited to the thirty- or forty-second sound byte. If media coverage is your prime reason for the speech, you might consider making only a statement to the press. Many executives go this time-saving route today.

YOUR BEST BET MAY BE THE TALK SHOW

You've seen and heard a good many of the hundreds, perhaps even thousands, of talk shows throughout the world on television and radio. It's pretty hard to miss them: they're all over the place. Note, though, that the talk show has one overriding format. Each show appeals to a specific type of audience. Whereas the news show sound byte is more inclined to have mass appeal, the typical talk show usually caters to a particular type of guest interview. By now you know why: they try to give their specific audience what that audience wants to hear and see.

Perhaps you've noticed that even news shows look and sound a lot like talk shows these days, but note that interviews on news shows are generally geared to the mass audience, interviews that interest almost everyone.

Determine in Advance What the Show Is All About

If you are interested in getting an interview on a local or national talk show, you must offer the producer a subject that appeals to the particular audience. How do you learn what the audience wants? Watch the show. Note the sort of interviews they regularly air. Become aware of the subjects discussed. In other words, you must become an expert on the show before you can hope to become a guest on the show.

In most cases, you are only one of several guests on a talk show, and what you have to say should be, if at all possible, dramatized in some fashion. A celebrity may get away with being only a "talking head," but when you're out to use airtime to promote something, a talk show host expects you to be entertaining and informative as well.

Decide What You Want to Say or Sell

What do you have to say? When it comes to business publicity, the important messages usually have to do with making your company, product, or service better known, giving them a good image, and preselling potential customers.

A lot of broadcast publicity is involved in news announcements. Perhaps you simply want to say that you are introducing a new product, holding a special event, or reporting on a major company move. These are all important, to be sure. You must know how best to handle these news stories, areas we cover later in this book. There is more you can do if you really want to give your company a public relations edge, something you can begin to prepare for right now.

Match What You Want to Say with What They Want to Hear

This is the secret of getting on talk shows. Once you have determined the type of interview subject most inclined to get a good reception from a talk show producer, set about getting ideas for making yourself and your subject acceptable.

For instance, this may be as simple as demonstrating a new product on the show, or if you plan a special event involving guest celebrities, booking one of the celebrities on the show for or with you to discuss the event and, of course, your company and/or product.

The Mechanics of Getting on a Talk Show

Once you have determined which television or radio interview show you wish to be on, call the station or network and ask for the show that interests you. Most talk shows have their own offices and telephone numbers or extensions. Once you reach someone in that office, ask to speak with the person who books the guests. This person is usually called the "booker."

There are a couple of ways you can go about this. You can speak with the booker in advance and then send the background information, which they most certainly will request, or you can send the background information first and then call to find out if they have time for you. I prefer the latter course. It takes less time, and you generally get a better reception. Be sure to send anything—stories, photographs, biography, or a sample of a product—that will help sell you and what you want to discuss.

Many but not all shows want a preinterview. Certainly the large network shows require this. In these preliminary interviews you get an idea of the type of questions you will be asked and any other details you should know in advance.

If you plan a travel schedule and want to set up interview shows along the way, do this well in advance, and once it is arranged, be sure to send a letter of confirmation.

Also, unless you are dripping with self-confidence, it might be a good idea to do your first couple of interviews on a small show on a small station.

TO WHOM DO YOU WANT TO SAY IT?

One trend in television programming—particularly cable—is toward producing shows that attract a specific audience—health shows, cooking shows, home repair shows, and so on. If you can identify a large audience (or market) you can usually find a network that appeals to it.

Make a list of television and radio shows that reach your audience: daytime, nighttime, women's shows, men's shows, sports, or news.

Study the shows you're aiming for in terms of time segments and types of interviews.

In addition to the major networks, don't forget the Financial News Network (FNN) and the twenty-four hour-a-day Cable News Network (CNN), as well as the myriad television and radio stations throughout the country.

YOU WANT SOME VISUALS TO BACK UP YOUR TV INTERVIEWS

Visuals may or may not be used, but be sure to provide samples of your product (if this is what you are promoting), a few color slides, and perhaps a good-quality videotape that helps document whatever it is you discuss on the show.

The Video Press Release Is Not a Home Movie

You've undoubtedly heard television stations suggest that you send in any home videos you might have on breaking news. This is to help them cover the 'hard news around town or around the country. The quality of these films is not nearly as important as the content.

There is a big difference between producing a good news show and producing a home movie. A good news video is not a home movie.

On the other hand, when it comes to promoting a company or product, the quality is important. Indeed, it is vital. I mean the quality of the content as well as the pictorial quality. There is today, however, a growing service industry that produces video press releases for a company or product. These are just as professionally produced as the shows on television. Indeed, they use only professionals to produce them. Then, once produced, the companies that provide this service send them out to television stations via satellite.

These services are mighty expensive and rarely for the beginner. Keep your eye on the future: maybe you'll need them at a later time.

CONSIDER THE PUBLIC SERVICE PROGRAMS

Television and radio stations have a certain amount of time that they must allot to public service programming. Keep in mind that you might be able to take advantage of this time simply by preparing a professional-quality film or video that is heavy on helpful information and very light on commercialism. About the only commercial you can expect is a line stating, "This film was produced by the Diggs Shovel Company." You might also find your way into this airtime by tying in with a nonprofit organization. Check this out as well.

CHAPTER PERSPECTIVE

In this chapter, we expanded the avenues available to you for publicity into the area of the electronic media. Regardless of the type of company publicity you need, refer back to this chapter to make sure you have utilized every possible means of getting your publicity seen and heard on television and radio.

Getting Publicity in the Business-to-Business Press

INTRODUCTION AND MAIN POINTS

In this chapter you will be introduced to business-to-business publications, usually referred to as trade journals. We explain not only what the trade journals cover, but also the reason they are so important to your plans for total company, product, and service publicity.

After studying the material in this chapter:

■ You will understand the services that trade journals provide to their readers and their importance to these readers.

■ You will discover how to select specific journals that deliver "hand-picked" audiences for your publicity.

■ You will be able to identify the seven basic types of trade journals available to you for publicity.

■ You will understand how best to give trade journal editors and readers the information they want and need.

■ You will learn how trade journal reporting differs from consumer reporting of your company news.

At a party recently, I spotted my usually withdrawn and dour friend talking with great animation to another guest. Curious as to what could possibly create such a sudden and dramatic change in a person, I edged over to where they were standing. What were they talking about? I couldn't make it out. To me it was a foreign language. All I knew was that they were discussing business—the very technical side of a business in which both of them were interested and involved.

Suddenly it occurred to me that when you talk with business people about their own businesses, you've got an interested, and I mean interested, audience.

This is what you do when you send a press release to a trade publication. You talk business to a business person about his or her own business.

When you tell them something that gives them an edge in a job or profession, they hang onto every word. As long as you feed them facts and details, they are content. This is the fascination of the business person for the trade journals in his or her own field. They speak the same language.

EACH INDUSTRY, PROFESSION, AND TRADE HAS ITS OWN LANGUAGE

Someone once said that if he had to briefly describe the language of the business press he would say, "It is the language used in everyday talk by people who know what they are talking about."

Almost every business-to-business publication has an established policy with respect to the industry language it uses—highly technical, semitechnical, or nontechnical—and this policy is determined by the preferences of their readers. Of course, every business journal is a technical paper to someone since it is concerned with the "techniques" of doing a job. When it comes right to it, the words *techniques* and *technical* when applied to language are simply words meaning "know-how."

As a rule of thumb, how technical should you get? Your study of the publication will tip you off. However, the best advice I can give you is to write your press releases in plain language, but don't shy away from technical terms if they are commonly used in the industry and they are essential to the story.

TRADE JOURNAL READERS WANT FACTS AND DETAILS

It doesn't take much imagination to realize that prospects want buying data—price shifts, new product information, merchandising techniques, and technical articles. Your sales message in many instances may be quite explicit simply because one purpose of the trade media is to impart information upon which intelligent buying decisions can be and are made.

You'll be happy to know that most trade journal readers generally sit still for a strong sales message. They want facts and details, regardless of how technical they are, and if this takes a lot of copy, so be it.

Also, when you introduce a new or improved product, it is always wise to prepare a fact sheet about the product for quick reference. This should cover, for example, all information carried in the new product announcement plus any other information you think is pertinent.

PROVIDE INFORMATION HELPFUL TO EDITORS AND READERS

Keep in mind that a trade journal is the major source of information for many business people. Consequently, to be helpful to the business journal you must be responsible for providing these editors and their readers with the news and information from your own company.

NEWS—THE MAIN THING

Most publications print news about new and improved products, new methods, processes, and techniques, new distribution plans and methods, new or renovated plants, new advertising and merchandising, new personnel—anything new that keeps readers up-to-date and especially that enables them to do a better job more easily and safely and, of course, make more profits.

Indeed, even the longer trade journal articles are usually handled as straight news, describing in plain language what some business or plant did. Many of them are illustrated with photographs.

TELL READERS WHAT THEY WANT AND NEED TO KNOW

Learn to identify with your customer. If you were the reader—the prospect—what would you want to know? In considering the best way to get publicity about your company and your product before a potential customer, try this. Try placing yourself in his or her shoes. Instead of the business you are in, try becoming someone considering the purchase of your product. Now as that potential customer, what information do you want? What information do you need to make an intelligent buying decision?

It may come as a surprise, but what you want to say is not always what the reader wants to hear. Sometimes we get so wrapped up in promoting ourselves and our own interests that we lose our objectivity and perspective. Although you may want to talk about the technological breakthrough of your product, your customer may want to know if your new component product fits on his or her old machine. You may want to brag about the architectural beauty of your new building, but your customer may want to know if it cuts down on delivery time.

DON'T JUST TELL THEM WHAT—TELL THEM WHY

Business journals want stories that educate. Don't tell them the mere fact it has happened. Tell them why—what it means to them and their jobs.

With the daily newspapers, television, and radio increasingly reporting the straight news about business, it obviously becomes pointless to report this same news up to a month later. It is therefore the job of the trade publication to interpret and analyze the news. You can help by giving the media the "why" behind any news you submit.

Readers also want to be shown new practices, not just told about them.

YOU CAN SHOW NEW PRACTICES THROUGH CASE HISTORIES

You will probably discover that your best publicity bet is to give readers very practical ideas and methods that worked for you, or one of your customers, and that they may be able to use. You may find that the journal may prefer a profile of an entire plant—yours or a customer's—or it may be that most of the stories are limited to one machine. Do your own exploring of the editors' preferences.

TODAY, A TRADE PUBLICATION CAN DELIVER A HAND-PICKED AUDIENCE

A successful business person I know recently wrote to a trade publication requesting a subscription. She enclosed a check. Within a week she received from the publisher a form letter asking her to send in some sort of printed matter—business card, appointment card, letterhead, or invoice—identifying herself in the field covered by the publication. Since she was in a related area but not in that specific field, she enclosed her business card and included a letter giving what she considered valid reasons for subscribing. Her subscription was rejected; her check returned.

A subscription rejected? A check returned? What could possibly possess a publisher to reject a subscription and return a check?

A very good one. A publication today must prove that it has not only the amount of circulation but also the type of circulation it claims. Annual circulation audits by the Audit Bureau of Circulations (ABC) and the Business Publications Audit of Circulation, Inc. (BPA) ensure this. If a trade publisher says it has circulation only among industrial plant managers, executives, distributors, and buyers, there had better be documentary evidence to back up this claim.

THIS WASN'T ALWAYS THE CASE

Today, when a trade publication claims to cover a field, it means it. This was not always true. Indeed, there was a time when, to sell advertising, media representatives are said to have jacked up their circulation figures anywhere from 100 to 250% over the actual numbers. This also meant that the type of circulation they claimed was suspect as well. Advertisers never really knew what they were buying. Something had to be done.

That "something" was done in 1914 when the Audit Bureau of Circulations was founded. This audit bureau was financed by publishers, advertisers, and advertising agencies. About fifteen years later, the Business Publications Audit of Circulation, Inc. was formed to concentrate on the auditing of business-to-business publications. There are others, too, each specializing in specific areas of the publishing field. Today at least one annual media circulation audit protects both the publishers and the advertisers.

EVERY BUSINESS HAS ITS "BIBLE"

Since you are in the business, you probably already know which trade journals are indispensable to you and your customers or prospective customers. Your first job in getting publicity is to begin studying that particular publication from a different point of view. Instead of reading it only to find out what others in your field are doing, begin analyzing it in terms of what the journal reports and why. Now, consider just what about your company's business, your products, or your services might fit into this editorial policy. This is an interesting challenge and one that can make a considerable difference in your company's business.

NOW, CONSIDER OTHER FIELDS AS POTENTIAL CUSTOMERS

This thought may have skittered around in your brain before now, but don't wait any longer to pin it down. Begin immediately to identify every other branch of industry, profession, or whatever that might conceivably use your product or service. Use your imagination.

Once you have come up with other possible areas of use, you have automatically come up with areas of additional publicity. Remember, each field has its own trade journals. Find our what these are. There are thousands of trade publications out there. Consider getting publicity in as many as you can.

KEEP IN MIND THAT THERE ARE MANY TYPES OF BUSINESS JOURNALS

Someone has said, "Hockey players don't hang around with chess players." This is why there is a need for so many business publications.

There are seven basic types of business-to-business publications. You must determine which most closely fit your needs and are most likely to reach your prospects—perhaps some you haven't even considered previously. Consider them now.

Trade

Trade magazines, using the term in the most restricted sense, go to retailers who are engaged in the resale of your products or who may use your products. Some of the stories they might be interested in include unusual store displays of your product—displays they can use in their own stores—successful sales campaigns, that sort of thing.

Industrial

Industrial magazines go to other producers: manufacturers and factories. Consider the factories and manufacturers that might use your product, producers you might not have considered before now. If your product can help them achieve better or greater production, tell them. Also, manufacturers are interested in stories about how your plant or product helped solve an industry problem related to them or how your product performed in production. Check these publications for more story and picture ideas.

Professional

Professional magazines go to doctors, dentists, engineers, and architects, as well as other highly educated, skilled professionals or industry experts. If your product could be used by any of these professionals or if your product might be recommended by them for use by others, review these professional publications.

Technical

Technical publications are primarily in such fields as electronics, communications, engineering technology, and electricity. A journal is classified as technical if it stresses editorially the latest techniques in a specialized field. These publications are interested in scientific and technical articles on new discoveries in chemistry, physics, or biology. Keep in mind while planning your publicity for these journals that even though they are technologically oriented, you must relate your product or service to the readers' needs, particularly how it affects a job or product.

Combination Vocational-Management Publications

You can reach management-level people in almost any field, but each publication is edited for a particular management sector. A study of this type of publication gives you publicity ideas you might use.

Institutional

Hotels, clubs, hospitals, and clinics and sanitariums, plus many other institutions, are the targets for institutional magazines. If your product or service can be applied to any facet of these institutions and their functions, the magazines in this field are excellent for you.

Farm

If your product or service has anything to do with rural life, you will find that you must be very specific about which division of farm specialization is closest to your product needs. Some of the subdivisions of farm journal publishing include agricultural equipment, crops and soil management, dairy farming, livestock, management, and regional and rural living. You'll probably find others.

NOW, SELECT SPECIFIC PUBLICATIONS FOR YOUR PUBLICITY

There are thousands of business, professional, technical, and industrial publications. Don't let the numbers distract you. Remember that each publication has carved out a market niche for itself. All you need to concentrate on are those few journals that can help you sell your specific product or service. The trick is to find those publications that meet your sales needs. Here's how you go about it.

Once you have identified a trade classification into which your product or service fits, obtain the audit reports on those publications. Remember, these audit reports tell you precisely the market niche each serves.

How You Can Get Audited Circulation Information

The Standard Rate & Data books covering the media are indispensable when you want this information. If your advertising department doesn't have a set of these books, you can probably find them in your library. If you are interested in a particular publication, you can contact the publisher directly for information about the circulation. As a potential advertiser, most publishers will send you a media kit, general background information on the publication, and a copy of the audit report. If you are interested in receiving audited circulation figures on several business-to-business publications, consider becoming a member of one of the audit bureaus. The cost is not all that high, and it might be worth it.

Study Your Selected Publications Carefully

It is vitally important that you get a copy of your target publication. You can usually get at least one copy by contacting the publisher directly. However, if not, check with your library.

Concentrate particularly on the sort of articles, short items as well as longer stories, they use. You won't have to read many issues to give you a good idea of the sort of information a journal prefers.

HOW TO GET A STORY IN A TRADE JOURNAL

Straight news items, such as announcements, should be sent on a regular basis whenever there is something pertinent to announce. If you want to submit a special article, you must send a query letter to the editor.

Remember: send your query to only one editor at a time, and this query should be written especially—and only—for that editor and that publication. Obviously, the query letter you send to a farm publication is not at all appropriate to an electronics publication, even though the product is the same.

Come up with the answers in specific terms of the "pitch" in each field.

If you have done your research thoroughly enough, you don't need to be reminded about how different each journal is and that each query letter—certainly each submission—must be tailored to fit the specific requirements of a specific journal.

How to Write It

Whenever possible, begin with the news element of the story and apply it to the specific audience. Remember, trade journal readers are busy people. They want ideas, and they want them fast. Keep your sentences and paragraphs short. Give them facts and details related as simply as possible.

When to Send Photographs

Well-planned and executed photographs taken to explain a subject with greater clarity are always welcomed by an editor. Remember, photographs should be 8 × 10 inch glossy prints showing as much detail as possible.

TRADE PUBLICITY—IS IT WORTH THE EFFORT?

You bet it is. It has been reported that more than half the goods sold in the United States are sold business-to-business. Indeed, it may be that the only customer for your product or service is another business.

Unit Purchases Are Much Larger

If you sell candy bars, you have to sell a lot of them to make a profit. You can do this either through the consumer media, which have enormous circulations, or through a trade journal that reaches the retail buyers of candy, for instance for a chain of stores.

Although relatively few prospects read trade journals, it stands to reason that unit purchases are generally much greater than most purchases developed by the consumer media.

This is especially true when it comes to industrial publications. A single sale might bring in enough cash to set you up for months.

Trade Journal Publicity Has a Long Life

Trade journal subscribers usually maintain a complete file of the publication to which they subscribe and continually refer to back issues for facts and further information. If the company has a business reference library, a file is generally kept for future reference. In most cases the files are kept around for years. This means that the publicity about your business, product, or service can be read years after you submitted it.

Trade Publications Generally Have Multiple Readerships

Subcriptions to business-to-business publications are often paid for by the company instead of the individual, in which case a single copy is routed to all interested employees in the organization. Consider, therefore, the number of influential people in a single company who have been exposed to your publicity. This enables you to reach every member of a decision-making team with a news release in any given issue.

CHAPTER PERSPECTIVE

In this chapter, we explained the importance of trade journals in terms of both extended publicity life and the size of unit purchases. We hope you now include business-to-business journals in all your product, service, and company publicity to achieve the maximum news and feature coverage for your company.

Dealing with the Press During a Crisis

INTRODUCTION AND MAIN POINTS

In this chapter we will help you learn how to prepare to deal with the press during a crisis, long before a crisis occurs. Although there are no hard and fast rules, we will give you guidelines recommended by many of the business people who have gone through the fire of crisis publicity.

After studying the material in this chapter:

■ You will learn how best to prepare today for a possible crisis tomorrow.

■ You will learn the questions you should be prepared to answer when the media arrive on the scene.

■ You will learn how best to express yourself to the media so there are no misunderstandings or repercussions.

■ You will learn how to keep abreast of fast-moving situations, as well as when and how to report them to the media.

Every day, it seems, another business faces a major crisis. Tonight it's a plane crash in which more than seventy people lost their lives. Last week it was an oil spill. A few weeks ago, a plant explosion released lethal gases into the atmosphere. You think to yourself, "Thank God we will never have to go through that."

Think again. No company is immune to crisis. True, yours may be an internal crisis of no interest to the media, but on the other hand, your crisis may involve the public. This is when it gets into the papers and on television and radio.

When public safety is involved, no company, large or small, is safe from the prying eyes of the media. If this should happen to you, how would you handle it? Are you prepared to cope with crisis? Are you prepared to cope with the media?

What would you do if, right now, your company faced a public-related crisis? What would you do if you left your office only to find yourself facing a dozen reporters with cameras, tape recorders, microphones, and pencils poised. What would you do if they fired questions at you—questions to which you have no answers?

If you are like most people, you'd probably get rattled, miffed, perhaps even angry. But this reaction would be a big mistake.

KEEP YOUR EMOTIONS IN CHECK

As you face the media during a crisis, just remember that every camera, every microphone, and every pencil is just waiting for you to show some emotion. After all, raw emotion is the essence of drama, and drama sells papers and raises ratings. Protect yourself and your company. Answer every question calmly. Even though beneath that poised facade you may be anxious and scared, never let it show. Never let yourself be needled into the headlines.

WHAT TO DO WHEN THE TELEPHONE RINGS AND ANNOUNCES A CRISIS

You are a small company that manufactures baby cribs — certainly a nonlethal product if ever there was one. You're safe from the possibility of a public crisis: right? Wrong.

Suddenly the telephone rings. It is a newspaper reporter. They have just been told that a child was injured by a crib you manufacture.

You don't believe it. No crib of yours could possibly hurt a child. You dismiss the call as a prank. Then the phone rings again. This time it is a television reporter. She wants to come over and get a statement from you. Suddenly, the realization sweeps over you that this isn't a hoax after all. What do you do now?

First, Gather the Facts

It may be that you must get the first facts from the media—facts about who was injured, how he or she was injured, and how badly. You also want to know, immediately, where and how to reach the family. You must check the facts. Perhaps the report isn't true or perhaps the incident has been exaggerated.

You investigate and find out that the child is in the hospital in a distant city. You call the hospital and speak with the doctor.

Good grief! The child was almost strangled. You can't figure out how this could possibly happen. The doctor relates to you what the mother told him. You are dumbfounded.

Immediately you order crib samples sent to your office. You call for the people involved in the making of the cribs, from the designer to the factory foreman. You also call your attorney.

Like a Monday morning quarterback, you now can see how an accident like this could happen. A child large enough to stand up in the crib could actually be hurt, or even killed. You are shocked.

Then you realize that two models of the crib have this same design. You obtain both model numbers.

Next you call the sales manager and get a list of every location where these cribs have been sold and shipped.

The Media Become Your Allies

Suddenly you realize that the media are not your enemies. You need the press to help you reach the parents all over the country who have purchased these cribs. You call a press conference to ask their assistance. You call every newspaper and television and radio station; you even call the wire services to come over immediately. Common sense begins to take over. You must alert others to the dangers of this crib before some other child is either hurt or, God forbid, killed.

THIS STORY IS REAL

Actually I don't know that the details are precisely as I have given them. All this is speculation. The substance of the story is true. Do you know how I know? I read a story about this in a newspaper several years ago. Although I am using fictitious names, the story read as follows:

PARENTS WARNED OF CRIB DANGER

The ABC Crib Company, of South Carolina, is trying to locate owners of two models of its cribs—the Baby Boom and the Infant Home—which could cause strangulation of infants old enough to stand.

Owners should immediately unscrew the top ornamental parts of the cornerposts and call the manufacturer collect for a modification kit at (telephone number), or write the ABC Crib Company (address).

Despite efforts to locate the cribs, there are still about 170 of the Baby Boom cribs and an undetermined number of Infant Home cribs in the New York area. The model numbers are:

What is your reaction to this story? Are you thinking, that's a terrible company? I'd never do business with them? Or are you thinking, this company, this owner, really cares about their customers . . . they accept the responsibility . . . they are doing everything possible to ensure the safety of the customers despite that it might do irreparable damage to the company.

I suspect that you feel only admiration for the company and its owner. I certainly do.

MANAGING NEGATIVE INFORMATION
Every crisis is unique, of course. But there are certain tactics that will work in almost any situation.

First, Get the Facts
Do whatever you have to do to get the necessary information. If you have to get it from the press, then do so. If you can get it from a customer, then do it. Get every detail about the product that has contributed to the damage. Get hold of your engineer, your designer, your factory foreman, your attorney—anyone it takes to get this information and find out what can be done about it. Never face the media unprepared.

Be Prepared to Answer Questions
There's no way of pinning down every question you might be asked because every crisis is different. But there are basic questions that every good reporter will ask:
- What happened?
- Is public safety involved?
- Were there any casualties?
- Who is affected: employees, customers, stockholders, the general public, children?
- When did it happen?

■Where did it happen?
■Why did it happen? What caused it?
These questions may come in any order, but be sure to have answers to all of them, or have a good reason for not having the answers.

Tell It All and Tell It Fast

This is not my advice alone. This is the advice of the majority of CEOs and public relations professionals who have been through a corporate crisis. Telling it all and telling it fast achieves several goals. First, you cut down on the coverage of the story. Everything goes into the first report and leaves little or nothing to be reported the next day. Second, it lessens the fear created in the public mind. It is well known that the less we know about a dangerous situation, the more we fear. Finally, telling it all and telling it fast presents your company in the best possible light during difficult circumstances.

Early in 1990 the Mecklenburg County Environmental Protection Department found that Perrier's bottled mineral water caused a "blip on the screen," indicating that the product contained benzene, a carcinogen. This was certainly a crisis for Perrier. Their reaction? An immediate and total recall of the product, with each step from its recall to its subsequent return to the shelves, fully reported to the media by Perrier and by the media to the public.

At this writing, Perrier is selling briskly once again with its reputation for product purity intact. The prompt actions of Perrier's executives and the attending publicity assured the company and product of this.

BE PREPARED

If you are the chief executive officer of a small hospital, would you ever imagine that you might have to contend with hundreds of victims at the same time? This is exactly what happened recently when a plane crashed in a small Upstate New York community. Fortunately, the hospital was prepared for just such a disaster. They had what they called a level 1 trauma system. They put this into effect immediately. Everyone in the hospital knew exactly where they should be and what they should be doing should a disaster strike. They had rehearsed over and over, despite the fact that they never expected anything serious to really happen.

You Should Have Your Own Level 1 Trauma Plan

Once you have studied all the problems endemic to your industry, and to business in general, especially those that could happen in your company, set up a team that can respond to these emergency situations. The plan should be flexible because no emergency is precisely as you might imagine it. Public relations people call this a response team. You are lucky. You have time to plan and rehearse.

When You Are Ambushed by the Media

Whether you are ambushed outside your home or in front of your office building or your office door, tell the media what you know for a fact—and only the facts—at this precise moment. Then explain that you are in the process of collecting more facts, and as soon as you get them, you'll tell the press everything. If you are sincere, they'll know. You can't put much over on the media.

Keep Abreast of Fast-moving Situations

Your response team should be available at a moment's notice during a crisis for the simple reason that bits and pieces of information can come in at any time and you must be ready to make decisions and coordinate companywide activities.

During these crisis meetings you should also discuss what information will be presented at the next news briefing and how it should be presented.

Use News Briefings to Provide Regular Updates

You may find it necessary to hold news briefings once or twice a day. The first news briefing should be held as early in the day as possible so that the media can make its deadlines. Also, be sure to anticipate—and be prepared to discuss—the questions that good journalists continually ask themselves:

- Where does the story go next?
- What questions remain unanswered?
- What new puzzles remain to be solved?

Be Open and Honest with the Media

It's the rare person who, during a business crisis, doesn't consider trying to cover up information that tends to make the company look bad. After all, it's really none of their business, is it?

Cover-ups are a mistake. A "no comment" or a mysterious silence only fires the imagination. If the crisis involves the public, it is the business of the media to find out all they can, with or without your cooperation.

Always keep in mind that you are not the media's only source of information. If you don't give them the information they'll get it from someone else, and you won't get first shot at telling your side of the story.

If there is something you don't know, say so. Tell them you're in the process of gathering even more information and will keep them informed. Then do so.

Express Yourself Very Carefully

Answer questions in as brief a manner as possible without leaving out any pertinent facts. This is no time to be creative. Reporters are waiting for a phrase that will make a colorful headline or that can be used out of context to create more problems.

If you plan a specific responsive action, say so, and explain why. If you do not plan to act, say so. Explain why.

Again, explain all technical terms in lay language. The greater understanding the reporter has of the situation, the more intelligently he or she will cover the story.

Always remember, express yourself calmly even though you may be tired, angry, and under stress.

When to Say "No Comment"

Preferably never. Consider your own reaction when someone says this to a reporter. Because we are human, most of us immediately think the worst.

There are exceptions, of course. If you know for a fact that the question is meant to embarrass you or if the reporter has a reputation for zingers, then "no comment" might be the safest route. Sometimes, too, there are valid legal reasons for refusing to comment. These reasons had better be strong, though, because from a public relations viewpoint it is always wise to keep the public—through the reporter—fully informed.

If you are suspected of holding something back, this usually serves only to intensify and lengthen media coverage.

Never Think of a Reporter as Your Confidant

There is something reassuring about being on friendly terms with a reporter. Some reporters, however, use their so-called friendship to get more information. All too often this works.

A good interviewer knows that a confiding tone of voice and the accompanying body language is one of the best methods available for getting a guest to open up and tell all. Be aware of this ploy. Remember, there is a big difference between being candid and being confidential. When you reveal your innermost secrets—worse, the innermost secrets of your business—you virtually give away the store.

It's always a good idea to establish ground rules, not only when you are about to be interviewed, but also when you talk informally with a journalist. Don't bet your life on confidentiality. If you want to be on the safe side, never discuss anything with a reporter that you don't want to see or hear in the media.

The whole life of a journalist is given to collecting facts. The responsibility is to the reader. As a thinking business person, you will agree that this is the best policy. Just remember that anything a journalist learns, regardless of how the information is obtained, belongs first to the reader. The role of confidant is just another way of getting that information.

Keep Sensitive Documents Out of Sight

A reporter once told me that she had mastered the art of reading documents upside down on the desks of the people she interviewed. She was proud of it. I have learned since that this practice is not uncommon. So, keep your desk clear of anything you don't want a reporter to read.

Accompany Reporters While They Are on the Premises

Keep in mind, yet again, that it is the job of reporters to get information any way they can. This means interviewing anyone they might run into while roaming through your offices or plant. Unless you have the happiest and most discreet employees in the world, you'd be wise to stick closely to reporters while they are on the premises.

CHAPTER PERSPECTIVE

In this chapter, we tackled the problem of dealing with adversity. Here we looked at the kinds of problems other companies have encountered and how they coped. We hope you have learned how to use all the publicity suggestions given in previous chapters to properly handle the dispersement of news during a disaster.

Making the Press Conference Work for You

INTRODUCTION AND MAIN POINTS

This chapter teaches you how to make a press conference or news briefing an effective and safe tool of publicity, stressing preparation—and more preparation.

After studying the material in this chapter:

■ You will learn how to determine whether you should consider holding a press conference.

■ You will learn how to prepare for a successful press conference or news briefing.

■ You will learn how to get maximum and positive results from a press conference.

■ You will understand the importance of planning for "damage control."

In a moment of enthusiasm and self-confidence, a business acquaintance of mine recently called a press conference. He considered himself lucky because it turned out to be a slow news day and he got a good media turnout. After the press arrived, he entered the room and seated himself at the table before several microphones.

He made his announcement—then came the questions. At first the questions were easy. He was obviously delighted at being at the center of the media's attention. Mentally he began preening himself. Suddenly he started getting the hard questions. He wasn't prepared for this. He got more and more flustered and began expressing himself imprecisely. He soon began talking himself into embarrassing corners and what began as a business promotion turned into a promotional disaster.

My friend learned a tough lesson that day: in a press conference, that's not an ordinary chair up there—it's a hot seat.

SHOULD YOU EVEN CONSIDER HOLDING A PRESS CONFERENCE?

Of course you should. You didn't get this far by being "chicken." As a general rule I suggest that you not hold any more press conferences than are absolutely necessary. Maintaining a good public image for your company is tough enough without going out of your way to look bad.

I don't mean to scare you off—just to alert you to the fact that although a press conference can be a terrific public relations tool, it can also subject you to unnecessary risks. As one old-time public relations expert advised his clients: "Nine times out of ten it is wise to send a press release instead."

NEVER UNDERESTIMATE A REPORTER

It is true that except for some specialists from the trade media, most reporters are generalists and consequently might ask questions that you think lack any understanding of the subject. Don't kid yourself, and don't dismiss their questions lightly. These artless questions might reveal a lack of knowledge about your particular subject, but this doesn't make them stupid. Every good journalist knows how to ask tough, penetrating questions even on subjects about which they may know very little. If you don't remember this, you're likely to find yourself in an awkward situation.

More important, unless you can explain your subject in such a way that all the reporters can clearly understand it, you take a serious chance of having your words misunderstood and, therefore, publicly misinterpreted.

HOW TO DETERMINE WHEN A PRESS CONFERENCE IS A GOOD IDEA

Keep in mind that reporters and editors are very busy people. They have other important stories to cover. They have newspapers to put out and newscasts to prepare. As in most businesses, there are rarely enough time and enough people to go around. News professionals simply don't have time to waste on a conference about routine information that could easily have been conveyed in a release or background memorandum. Calling an unnecessary or nonsubstantive news conference damages your credibility. The press may not respond to future invitations.

When you consider having a press conference, ask yourself these questions:

▬ Is the subject or product of wide enough interest?

▬ Is the topic or product of major news value?

▬ Is the subject of such a controversial nature that it demands give-and-take to express your message fully?

▬ Is the new product so complex that a demonstration seems to be the only way to explain the essential facts?

▬ Is the new product so large that it cannot be demonstrated on a one-to-one basis?

▬ If you are announcing your company's earnings or a merger, acquisition, or move, will a press conference gain more credibility with the media if it is called immediately after an annual stockholders' meeting, or a meeting of the board of directors, when important and interesting people are available for interviews?

▬ Is news breaking so fast on a developing story that a press conference or a series of "news briefings" is the only way to keep the media up to date?

▬ Do you think that a frank discussion with the media is the only way to head off publication of partial truths about your company that are unflattering or perhaps even damaging?

In considering your answers, always keep in mind that the subject must be of strong enough interest to the media for them to arrange their schedules around it. Remember, you can call a news conference, but this doesn't necessarily mean that the press will show up.

HOW MUCH PREPARATION IS NECESSARY FOR A SUCCESSFUL NEWS CONFERENCE?

In the newspaper recently I read about how a top government official rehearses for a news briefing. It said:

"He is diligent, working 12 hours a day, preparing assiduously for his briefings and staying home most weeknights so that he will be sharp at the briefings." Despite this, the story continued, "he still garners a few complaints for laxness in checking his information."

Perhaps this sounds a bit extreme, but unless you are fully prepared, a news conference can be lethal. What you have to keep in mind is that what you see on television is only a few seconds of what usually takes days, perhaps even weeks, to prepare.

Even if you make all the necessary preparations, if you make a misstatement or stumble on the steps, this is probably what will be on television—not your message.

USE EVERY OPPPORTUNITY TO MEET THE PRESS—IN ADVANCE

Imagine, for a moment, standing before the press corps and everyone is a stranger. Now, imagine yourself standing before a group of men and women, some of whom have become friends, most of whom are at least speaking acquaintances. Which situation is less threatening? Under which set of circumstances do you think you'll get the better break? The most understanding? The answer, of course, is obvious.

This brings us to the first part of your preparation for a successful press conference: Get to know the press in advance. How do you go about this?

▬ Whenever a reporter calls for information, use this opportunity to get acquainted. Go out of your way to provide the information requested—plus. Become a valued "source."

▬ Always keep your door open to the media, literally and figuratively. Be available. Let them know they can visit you at will. Get acquainted on an informal basis when possible.

▬ Encourage them to ask questions, express any gripes they might have or have heard, and state their own opinions.

▬ Let them get to know, in advance, more about your company, your products, and your services. Then when the time comes they can write about your business with a greater depth of knowledge and understanding.

Just remember, no confiding!

STUDY MEDIA COVERAGE TO LEARN ABOUT MEETING THE PRESS

This is yet another instance of the media as your textbook. Hardly a day passes without someone being questioned by the media. It may be a formal press conference, it may be an informal news briefing, or it may be a push-and-shove interrogation by the press. Watch them all. When possible, tape them and study them over and over.

In each instance, place yourself in the position of the person being interrogated. Note the questions asked. Imagine yourself as both a willing and an unwilling target. What would you do? How would you handle yourself? What would you say?

HOW TO AVOID GIVING OUT CONFIDENTIAL INFORMATION

In most situations you can anticipate even the most awkward or embarrassing questions you might be asked. You should check out any legal ramifications with your attorney and discuss your answers with other experts and members of the management team.

In most instances it is advisable to answer a question as frankly and honestly as possible. If an answer at this time would be premature, say so. Explain why.

Sometimes the words "off the record" give you the freedom to discuss a situation without actually going public. Use this phrase with discretion. It won't work forever, and sometimes it doesn't work at all.

Another possible answer is that you don't have the information on hand but you'll get back to the reporter with the answer as soon as possible. Then, by all means, do get back.

The phrase "no comment" usually doesn't go down too well, so if possible try to avoid it at all costs.

TRY TO ANTICIPATE EVERY POSSIBLE QUESTION YOU MIGHT BE ASKED

During a press conference reporters are supposed to keep to the theme at hand, but have you ever known a pack of good reporters who always stick to the rules? In most instances they use the press conference to tap you for information on any subject related to your business, and you'd better be prepared to answer or have a mighty good reason for not answering.

Try to anticipate any question that might be asked, no matter how far out it might be. You can do this by inviting your peers and your friends and family to ask you questions about your business—no holds barred. If there is any question you can't answer, make a note to find the answer.

Be sure to include some bright questioners who know nothing about your company or your subject. Let them ask questions until they truly understand what you're talking about. It might even be a good idea to make tape recordings of these sessions so you know precisely which of your explanations clarified the point. Also, make a note of the questions you were not able to answer to their satisfaction, and then work on the answers.

Be sure to define all technical jargon and eliminate all professional buzzwords. There is no place in a news conference for vagueness.

PRACTICE BEFORE YOUR PEERS

Prepare your material, and then get up before your peers—the most professional and knowledgeable people you know in the field—and allow them to critique everything you present.

Be sure that your legal advisors and technical experts are on hand as well to check out your answers.

We hope that by the time you get to the press conference you will feel and be a self-assured and competent performer.

SURROUND YOURSELF WITH EXPERTS

At the same time that you should translate technical jargon into lay language for the uninitiated, you must also be prepared to provide any trade journal reporters present with more details and more technical facts.

You've probably noticed that at televised press conferences, when a very touchy or technical topic is discussed, there are always experts nearby who, often unasked and unannounced, move into camera and microphone range and answer a specific question.

Take heed. Whenever technical or legal points are involved, be sure to have technical experts and counsel present and primed to give prompt, brief, and understandable answers.

KEEP THE PRESS CONFERENCE ORDERLY

There is an accepted procedure for press conferences.

■ The spokesperson usually reads a brief statement regarding the reason for the conference.

■ Reporters are recognized for questions by the spokesperson, who may have one or two experts nearby to assist with highly technical queries.

■ One follow-up question is usually permitted.

■ Professional standards require reporters to confine their questions to the issue.

■Unlike the very important and formal press conference that ends when the senior reporter present (in terms of experience, not age) rises and says, "Thank you, Mr. President," the business news conference generally ends less formally, for example when a staff member reminds the spokesperson that the allotted thirty minutes is up.

PLAN FOR DAMAGE CONTROL

Even when you follow the standard procedure for conferences, an element of the unpredictable is always involved. Here are methods to avoid potentially troublesome moments. This is called "damage control."

■Schedule press conferences infrequently.

■Slow the pace of questioning by lengthy answers.

■Refuse to be drawn into an argument or debate.

■Refrain from making any unflattering side remarks. They are sure to be picked up by someone.

■Try to keep the meeting to no more than thirty minutes.

■Begin on time. End on time.

■Once it's over, get out of there! Don't hang around after the meeting is closed—and it's not over until you're out of sight and sound.

■If one reporter is intent on speaking with you after the meeting, keep it short. You are on solid ground here because it is considered unethical for one reporter to remain after the others have gone so he or she may conduct a private conference with the spokesperson.

MAKE ARRANGEMENTS WELL IN ADVANCE

Someone said recently, "We do all the planning and he gets all the headlines." Well, someone has to do a lot of planning before any press conference if it is to be successful.

Among other things, you select the best date, day of the week, and hour for the press conference. You must have a good location, and you must have plenty of written backup for the media.

Select the Best Day

Once you believe you have an announcement that will interest a wide and general audience, select a day and date that give you the best chance of a good media turnout. Generally the best days for a well-attended press conference are Tuesday through Friday.

Check the media carefully for any upcoming news event that may provide you with competition. This includes visiting celebrities and major sports events.

Choose the Best Hours

The best hours are those that fit best not into your schedule, but into the schedules of the media. As a general rule the hours from 2:30 to 4:30 p.m. are good, but check with the media in your own community. The important thing is that the print media get the story in time to hit both the late editions of the evening papers and the early editions of the morning papers. You also want to finish in time so that the story makes the evening news shows.

Be Prepared with Written Backup

If you call a press conference to announce anything from a new product to a major merger, it is essential to have written backup information available to each reporter. This can be anything from a one- or two-page news release to a well-packed press kit containing news and feature stories and background material, as well as photographs, covering every aspect of the subject.

Be sure to have your news release or press kit delivered to the editor of any of the media not represented at the press conference.

On the morning before the press conference, have an advance news release delivered to each invited guest with the release date reading (for example):

FOR RELEASE AFTER 4:30 P.M. WEDNESDAY, APRIL 15

HOW TO INVITE THE PRESS

Just how you invite the media to your press conference often depends on the importance of the announcement and the amount of lead time you have before the conference. If possible, send the invitation a week in advance.

■ For most press conferences, send a one-page memo to a specific and appropriate editor informing that editor of the day, date, time, place, and subject of the press conference. The usual format is:

EVENT: Introducing our new Back to Basics Promotion
WHERE: Diggs Shovel Company, (Address)
WHEN: Wednesday (Month Date)
TIME: 2:30 p.m.
CONTACT: John Diggs, (000)000-0000

▬If you will make a major announcement, a much more formal invitation is usually expected. Your invitation should contain all pertinent facts about the purpose of the press conference, the time, place, speakers, and so on. Send your invitation to the most appropriate editor, say the business editor or news editor, who will probably assign a reporter and/or photographer.

▬When the need for a press conference comes up suddenly, a telephone call suffices. As stated before, this is generally called a news briefing.

CALL THE PRESS THE DAY BEFORE THE PRESS CONFERENCE

It is usually a good idea to call all those you have invited to the press conference two or three days after you sent out your release just to make sure they received it and to get an estimate of who plans to attend.

The day before or the morning of the conference, check again by telephone to remind each invited guest of the day and time of the press conference.

MAKE SURE YOU HAVE A PROFESSIONAL PHOTOGRAPHER ON HAND

Make sure a professional photographer is available to take specific photographs requested by members of the press. Someone who understands the product might be available to answer questions and help set up the pictures.

HAVE SOMEONE AVAILABLE TO ASSIST NEWS PHOTOGRAPHERS

Television and newspaper photographers may want exclusive picture setups. See to it that someone is available to round up the requested individuals for the pictures and, if it is a new product introduction, to make sure that the new product is adequately and properly displayed. Accurate caption material should also be provided to photographers.

BE SURE TO HAVE PLENTY OF CHAIRS AND GOOD AUDIO EQUIPMENT

Be sure to have plenty of chairs and, if necessary, good audio equipment so that each member of the press can be comfortable while taking notes. Everyone should be able to see and hear the talks and see the demonstrations easily.

CHAPTER PERSPECTIVE

In this chapter, we tried to make you feel more confident and comfortable about dealing with the media during a press conference. We tried to steer you clear of damaging statements and actions so that the media become allies instead of threats.

How to Plan and Promote a Special Event

INTRODUCTION AND MAIN POINTS

This chapter pinpoints the reasons that special events are often so important to a company's overall publicity program. We explain how to come up with special event ideas, and we offer some ideas and idea starters for your own special events. You will also learn how you can use local, national, and international anniversaries and special occasions as pegs for special event publicity.

After studying the material in this chapter:

▬ You will learn why special events are often necessary.

▬ You will learn what elements must be incorporated into a special event to capture the maximum media publicity.

▬ You will learn how to tie in your special events with calendar events, seasons, fads, and other topical and timely occasions.

▬ You will learn how you can initiate special event publicity through giving.

▬ You will learn how to use your company's special occasions for a series of special events.

▬ You will learn why it is imperative to get publicity in advance, during, and after each special event.

Early one morning while walking the dog I noticed, out of the corner of my eye, what appeared to be a white flash from across the street. I looked in that direction but saw only dark windows in the townhouse of a friend. Suddenly I saw the flash of white again. It came from the second-floor window. It was my friend waving to me. I couldn't see her at all. All I could see was the movement of her hand. I waved back.

This is what a special event is to a business. It is the act that attracts attention.

Your attention-getting special event may indeed be as subtle, warm, and friendly as a good-morning wave—

perhaps something like homeless puppies playing in your store window as they wait to be adopted. On the other hand, the best special event for you might be as spectacular as a Fourth of July fireworks display or a Macy's Thanksgiving Day parade.

ARE SPECIAL EVENTS NECESSARY?

No, not always. Special events are for special purposes. If you need to increase traffic in your store, a special event can help you do this. If you need to increase product sales, a special event can help you. If you need to improve your company image within your community or industry, a special event can help. Whatever it is you need to accomplish, it's very likely that you can create a special event to help you do it.

SPECIAL EVENTS ALSO FILL NEWS GAPS

Few companies can naturally generate news every day or even every week. If your special need is to keep the name of your company, product, or service before the public, then a series of special events may be your answer. Special events are very effective tools of publicity. You should learn to use them.

BE SURE TO INCORPORATE THE ELEMENT OF NEWS

We keep going back to this because this is what publicity is all about—generating news. Otherwise, you may just as well have a sale and buy advertising to promote it.

If you want to get publicity, however, remember—you must make it newsworthy.

And, speaking of newsworthy, consider the story about Albert Eisele, the public relations consultant who "lured" Mikhail S. Gorbachev to Minnesota in 1990. Mr. Eisele had visited the Soviet Union in February 1987, and Control Data had sold computers to the Soviet Union since 1968.

An important public relations special event? You'd better believe it. How many times does a company get its name and product mentioned on the front page of any newspaper—let alone *The New York Times*? But this was just the beginning. Every day until long after Mr. Gorbachev has visited Minnesota the Control Data Corporation was in the forefront of the news.

YOU CAN START WITH A CALENDAR EVENT—A RED-LETTER DAY

There are lots of holidays, anniversaries, and, of course, historic birthdays. Which one should you choose? To make it easier, try to select an occasion that, in some way, you can relate to your product or service. It would, for instance, be easier and more appropriate on George Washington's birthday to promote cherries rather than peaches.

It is January and Benjamin Franklin's birthday is coming up on January 17. What is there in Franklin's life that relates to your product or service?

You find out by reading his biography or by checking the encyclopedia that Ben's father was a "tallow chandler." If you manufacture or sell candles you decide that for Ben's birthday you will decorate a huge birthday cake with enormous candles, or you can decorate it with 285 or 300 candles, depending upon how many years have passed since his birth in 1706. You add to the news interest, of course, if all the guests come to your party dressed in the costume of the day, or if all your guests are named Franklin.

This is not all. If you manufacture or sell sporting goods, you will be attracted to the fact that Ben loved sports, especially swimming. Do you make or sell anything related to water sports? In honor of Franklin's birthday you could hold a swimming competition. Bring in a famous swimmer or coach as a special guest to tout the benefits of swimming and other water sports, and the safety features. You can hold a swimsuit fashion show in January. Why not?

You remember that Ben Franklin became a printer. Printing—now this brings to mind such products as photocopy machines, offset, word processors, and Fax machines —another news peg for these products. You could set up an historical exhibition or book an expert to represent your company on television and radio interview shows.

Did you remember that Ben invented the closed stove? What a good time to tie in with this if you make or sell anything related to heating equipment. What about giving a modern stove for cooking or heating to a family in desperate need of one?

You remember that in 1752 Franklin made his memorable kite experiment, by which he demonstrated the electrical nature of lightning. If you sell electrical appliances, you could sponsor a kite-flying contest. Another "kite" tie-in is for a product whose feather-light weight is a significant sales message. You can attach your product to the tail of the kite and let it float away, and perhaps give something special, in addition to the attached product, to whomever retrieves the kite.

You find other things in Ben's biography, but you get the idea.

YOU CAN BEGIN WITH THE SEASON

What about the back-to-school migration? Let's say your product is a transportation item—trucks, autos, minibuses, even wagons. Just how can you tie in with a back-to-school promotion in such a way that it creates news? Think like this: In what way do students need transportation?

Why not create a caravan of cars to transport young students on the first day of school? You'll have the media climbing all over themselves for pictures of tiny children making their way to kindergarten.

If you are located in a college town, the local collegians moving onto campus usually have a moving day. Offer your services, but make sure that one of the students or instructors you "move" is someone with name appeal—the daughter or son of the mayor or governor, or the child of an actor or writer. There is your news picture.

BE ALERT TO BREAKING NEWS

When people are in trouble, they need help. When there is a community crisis, everyone needs to pitch in. When your product can be of help, you seldom need to ask for publicity—you'll get it naturally. This is the media's way of rewarding a Good Samaritan.

▬ During a blackout, you can provide portable lighting or refrigeration.

▬ During a flood, you can provide boats, shelter, food, clothes, pumps, and boots.

▬ For people without heat, consider giving out heaters, camping equipment, and warm clothing.

TIE IN WITH SOMETHING TOPICAL AND TIMELY

▬ John Diggs could select Arbor Day for a Diggs Plant A Tree Project using the Diggs shovel. He could give a Diggs shovel to anyone who will plant a tree, perhaps in an area set aside for the community project.

■ On the occasion of the United States and China forming a commercial bond, John Diggs can (tongue in cheek) set up a special event with Americans digging a hole clear through to China, and at the same time in China, a group of Chinese are trying to dig a hole through to the United States. Of course, both groups use Diggs shovels.

■ At the beginning of the baseball season, offer free eye tests for umpires.

■ To tie in with a citywide marathon, set up an emergency tent with appropriate first-aid products and services.

■ Summer coming on? Round up instructors in summer sports to give tips—using your sporting goods, of course.

CELEBRITIES MAKE NEWS

You don't always have to go it alone. Publicity people are always looking around for publicity tie-ins for their own clients and products. Say there is a new show in town—a theatrical production or a new movie. They want publicity as much as you do. Get together. Call the manager or the press agent and tell them how you figure your company or product fits into their own promotions.

■ You could invite the entire cast to your restaurant for dinner or, if you are publicizing a deli, you can send over a hero sandwich 15 feet long.

■ If, for example, you are publicizing a health club, invite visiting celebrities to work out as your guests while they are in town. Publicity people know the value of this: it is another free publicity opportunity to offer their clients and yet another means of getting free publicity for their own services.

■ Suggest holding an autograph session in your place of business. The more important or famous the person, the larger the crowd you get. The local media will want a biography and photograph of the person you are introducing to the public. This is sent to the local media with a news announcement giving the time and place of the event.

■ Well-known people are always traveling throughout the country promoting something or other, and they are often looking for a local "stage." You can provide one. If you read about someone of importance coming to your community, invite them to visit your place of business. The enticement might be a remote telecast or broadcast interview from your store (set up well in advance with a local interviewer, news editor, or disk jockey) or a press conference to which you invite all the local media.

■ A local disk jockey or interview personality might be delighted to conduct his or her interviews from your window or from a table in your store. In many instances these people feature interviews with visiting celebrities so you get a double-whammy promotion. Report in advance if there are any special guests, and certainly report that you are going to begin the series of broadcasts. Remember, the broadcaster is also a celebrity.

■ Photograph any and all celebrities, and feature them in your windows and on your walls.

EXPLOIT A FAD

When you spot a fad—go with it. When auctions are "in" offer your product for auction. When roller skates make the news, use roller skates and skaters in unexpected situations, perhaps delivering your product by skates. When a new game is the fad and someone in your company is an expert—or your product or company is related in any way to the new fad—get in on the act and hire experts to teach it, provide a facility where it can be played, or sponsor a citywide contest.

USE A LARGE COLOR TELEVISION TO COVER SPECIAL EVENTS

Few working people can get away during the day to watch really important special events on television. I've even seen a small stand in a railroad station gather hundreds of people around a television when a national news event was taking place.

■ Be sure to report to the news media that this service is available for those who want to take their "lunch hour" at the time of the event.

■ Of course, just keeping a large color television tuned to a popular station makes people stop and watch. I nearly broke my leg bumping into a fire hydrant while I tried to look at a show while passing a store window where a televised event was being aired. It attracts attention, that's for sure.

GIVE SOMETHING TANGIBLE TO THE COMMUNITY

When you give something away, especially to your community, this is definitely news to your local media.

■A clock company in Michigan contributed a clock tower to their community. You might offer your product to the city if it is the type of product that will improve the quality of life in your community: keep it cleaner, safer, or more beautiful.

■I read about a local garbage collector who chops up Christmas trees and offers the chips free to citizens for their gardens.

PROVIDE A NEEDED SERVICE

If you are interested in attracting the attention of people with pets or small children, provide a much-needed service. It doesn't take much imagination to know what that service might be.

■Consider babysitting the kids. One problem parents have when shopping is finding a place to park the children. If you have the space for a small nursery, decorate it attractively, bring in volunteers to take care of the children (mothers might trade off), and give the mothers time for a little freedom—to shop or dine in peace. Take pictures of the youngsters at play and send them to the media, but first be sure that each mother signs a picture release.

■A dog-walking or dog-sitting service will create a sensation. Pet owners are loyal friends if you love their pets. They'll do just about anything for those who do things for them to make their lives easier. There are so many places you can't take a pet these days that if you provide shelter and care for the pets while the owners dine or shop the word will get around fast. Also, animals provide fantastic picture possibilities.

■You can even use your walls to bring in traffic and customers. You can buy decorations for your walls, but why not use this space to give budding artists a place to exhibit their art? If the artist is rich, famous, or socially prominent, this adds yet another dimension to your publicity. Be sure to send out an announcement of each new exhibit, along with a biography of the artist. Hold a press showing each time you open a new show.

DO SOMETHING UNEXPECTED

I still remember the column note about a builder who constructed a prefab home for his bride—in six days! I even remember the name of the company and where it was located, just in case I ever need a house built in a week.

Was this special event effective? You bet it was. If I remember so much about it years later, surely many people were influenced by it. This was a special event that really paid off.

A COMPANY OCCASION CAN BE AN "EXCUSE" FOR MANY SPECIAL EVENTS

You are planning to construct a new office building. You have already announced this, and you figure this is about all you can do for now. Right? Wrong. You can use this as your excuse for a series of special events right up to and including your move into the new structure.

First, of course, you could have a ground-breaking ceremony with well-known personalities from the community, the industry, and perhaps even the entertainment world to generate even more publicity. You can hold a special ceremony around the laying of the cornerstone—placing into the cornerstone memorabilia that will be revealed in fifty or a hundred years. Then there is the topping-off ceremony, placing a tablet on the completed building, the dedication of the new building, the open house, and anything else you can think of. Each of these subsidiary events should get plenty of publicity before, during, and after the occasion. Now, try this technique of surrounding all your important company news with subsidiary events to get extra publicity.

GET PUBLICITY IN ADVANCE

Some special events need a great deal of advance publicity even to get off the ground. Merely staging something special won't do the trick unless you tell people it is going on. I'll never forget one occasion many years ago when the teenage department of a large local department store invited the leading disk jockey into the department. They were all geared for masses of teenagers to mob the place. Not a single teenager showed up. Why? Each person had depended on someone else to tell the teenagers—to get publicity for the event. No one had done it. It was humiliating for the disk jockey and nearly lost the account for the publicity agency. There is nothing worse than planning a special event and having no one show up.

In addition to advanced publicity about the event, be sure to invite the media. Prepare a press kit, and send it in advance. Call all those invited a day or so before the event to remind them or confirm their attendance.

GET ONGOING PUBLICITY

As we passed a famous manufacturing company recently, a friend and I stopped to take the company tour announced on a large sign near the highway. It was a fascinating tour, and there were, in the guest book, pages and pages of names of people who had taken it. The guide informed me, however, that virtually all their visitors consisted of people passing by or word-of-mouth publicity that brought in local people and their guests. They hadn't done anything since the first tour to get ongoing publicity. They hadn't done anything to use the tour to increase sales.

Don't merely give a tour—promote it. Let people know about it. It stands to reason that if the people don't know about you and your special event, they aren't going to make plans to be there. Consequently, any sort of publicity that tells the public you are in existence, that you have something special to offer, and where you can be found is of first importance.

■Get photos of visitors, and send them to their hometown papers.

■Invite visiting celebrities to take the tour, and make sure you notify the local press.

Send news releases to all the media you can find in your area, and don't forget even the smallest neighborhood papers or throwaways. Think saturation.

GET FOLLOW-UP PUBLICITY

A friend who was in charge of sales promotion for a national shelter magazine was recently reminiscing about the time she threw a party in the subway. It was for advertisers and potential advertisers. The media, of course, were invited. She had the subway station scrubbed down, flowers everywhere, and a bar set up. She had her guests picked up at different places by a bus. She said the whole thing was "super secret." No one knew where they were going. Then there appeared an antique subway car that transported all the guests to the Brooklyn Museum.

The next day, she said, the special event received seven inches of publicity space in a major local newspaper. Right next to it, she said, was an advertisement paid for by a competitor. It had cost $18,000.

Are special events worth the time and effort? You bet they are.

CHAPTER PERSPECTIVE

In this chapter we attempted to teach you a way of thinking to create special events—not just give you specific ideas for special events. We stressed the importance of allowing your product or service to dictate your promotion. We also explained how carefully selected special events can be utilized to accomplish specific public relations goals.

How Publicity Can Improve Your Product and Company Image

INTRODUCTION AND MAIN POINTS

In this chapter we will explain the importance of a good image to a company, product, or service and how to deal with the ways that publicity can help you improve it. We will explain how to determine the best image for your business and how to project that image to your various publics.

After studying the material in this chapter:

— You will learn what goes into creating a company image.

— You will learn how you can use publicity to help create a good image for your business.

— You will learn how to identify the best image for each of your target audiences.

— You will learn how to get publicity for a new trademark or package design.

A company whose skin care products I have used for years recently changed its package design. It was a considerable visual improvement. Usually I like such changes and improvements. The original package was old-fashioned, and I mean old-fashioned. It looked as if someone had simply licked the label and stuck it on the nearest bottle.

This change bothered me, though. Finally I figured out why.

This product was originally recommended to me by a doctor. Subconsciously, my perception of the product was one of a "prescription." Also, it gave me the feeling that I was one of the few "in the know." With the new package design, the product lost its image of "reliability," of "doctor-recommended," of "exclusivity." Suddenly, the prescription skin care product had become a cosmetic.

What does this have to do with publicity? Word-of-mouth publicity is about as effective as any publicity you can get, anywhere. In this instance the word-of-mouth publicity had come from a professional "who should know." It might just as well come from your neighbor, friend, or fellow dog walker. Regardless of where it comes from, when a positive image created by word-of-mouth publicity is changed, perhaps even damaged, the effect on sales can be serious.

WHY NOT CONVINCE YOURSELF?

Open your kitchen cupboard door and study the products on the shelf. Can you remember why you purchased each and every one of them the first time? Was it the advertising that influenced you? What about someone's recommendation? Was it a celebrity who gave a testimonial? What about news or feature stories you read in the newspapers or heard on television or radio? What about interviews with the company's representatives?

Now, consider the other things around your home—the carpeting, mattresses, furniture, radios, microwave, washing machine, refrigerator, stove—in each case try to remember what convinced you to buy that particular brand. It may surprise you.

NOW, PRETEND YOU ARE SHOPPING TODAY

You are interested in buying a type of product you have never bought before. There are several brands on the market, but since you have not tried any of them, you have no idea which of the half-dozen brands is the best. So how do you decide? How do you know which to buy? What is the influencing factor?

Have you ever heard about any of the products? Have you read about them? Does the name sound familiar? Does the trademark look familiar? You look for the name of the company that manufactures the product. Have you ever heard of the company? What sort of reputation does it have? Is it reliable? What about the package? Is it old-fashioned, or is it up-to-date and modern? Which image are you most comfortable associating with this type of product?

Companies are very sensitive to these questions and your answers. Many years ago I worked for an industrial design firm whose original owner and designer, Jim Nash, had been responsible for updating the packages of some of the most famous products around. One, in particular, I remember. It is that cheerful face on the Quaker Oats box. Originally, the entire head-to-toe figure of the Quaker man was displayed on the package. Little by little, the Quaker man seemed to come closer, until now only his face is portrayed. This was done to make the Quaker man appear friendlier and more accessible.

With each updating, there was a wealth of publicity. Each change was news. This was a product and trademark that people all over the country had grown up with.

One of the familiar personality images being used in merchandising today is on Famous Amos cookies. A picture of the cookie creator appears on every bag and tin. Because he wanted his image to be "natural, a part of my true personality, something that was me at any given time," the smiling Amos is shown wearing a Hawaiian-print shirt and straw hat. How much of an impact did this image have? Well, we have all read stories about Famous Amos in the press and, should you be so inclined, you can see Famous Amos' shirt and hat on display when you visit the Smithsonian Institution in Washington, D.C.! That made mighty good publicity, too, as you can well imagine.

Today, we are more apt to see logos—product or company names or initials—than portraits. It may be difficult to understand just why a certain typeface can create a specific image for a corporation, but try to imagine IBM printed in italics and perhaps you will get the idea. (You may recall when IBM adopted its present logo many years ago, it got a lot of press coverage.)

YOUR COMPANY AND PRODUCTS ARE JUDGED EVERY DAY

Your company name, your product names, and the reputation of both are some of the greatest assets of your company since every sale is influenced by a company's image.

The familiarity and reputation of its name is among the greatest assets of any company, whether it deals directly with the public or not. We are all influenced by reputation in choosing everything we buy and in every association we make.

The image of your company, product, or service can be quickly detected on the bottom line. This is why it is so important that you create, maintain, or improve a good image.

WHAT EXACTLY IS A COMPANY'S IMAGE?

A new client once said to me, "The first thing I want you to do is get a picture of our company."

This really stumped me. How in the world does one photograph a company? Do you take pictures of the building? Do you take snapshots of employees working at their desks? Do you take candid shots at parties? Do you get a portrait of the president or, perhaps, each of the executives? Do you take pictures of all the products? Do you grab a shot of the Dow-Jones quote at the end of a business day? If it is a global company, do you take photographs in the United States, England, France, Germany, Canada, Japan? Which? All?

THE BEST "PICTURE" IS AN IMAGE OR PERCEPTION OF THE COMPANY

Actually, the "picture" or "image" of a company is the sum total of all these things—and more. Everything and everyone connected with a company and its products or services contribute to the image. It is the creation of one picture at a time, verbal as well as visual, all of which are eventually blended into a single image in the public mind. Well, not exactly the public mind, more like your mind or my mind, since each of us has a different image of a company or product, depending upon our own personal experiences, preferences, and prejudices.

PUBLICITY HELPS CREATE ONE PICTURE AT A TIME

As you know by now, publicity uses every possible verbal and visual means to accomplish a public relations goal.

■ Take pictures of your new enlarged headquarters if you want to impress on your various publics that yours is a flourishing and successful company.

■ Take snapshots of employees working at their jobs if those jobs are unique to your particular company, product, or service.

■ Take candid shots at a party if you want to "humanize" a company with a cold and forbidding reputation.

■ Get a portrait of the president and other top executives if you want to show that you have the industry's top-notch personnel.

■ Take pictures of all your products if you want the good reputation of one product to rub off on all the others.

■Should yours be a global company, take photographs in countries all over the world if you want to tell your various publics about the worldwide acceptance of your company, products, or services.

Let's face it, the prestige provided by the right publicity not only can help you sell your products or services, but it can also attract dealers and the best employees, make the stockholders happy, provide protection from price-cutting competitors, and help you successfully introduce new products.

WHY PUBLICITY IS SUCH A POWERFUL IMAGE BUILDER

I'm not about to put down advertising, but it's the rare person who doesn't occasionally consider that advertising space is bought and paid for and that in advertising space a company can say just about anything it wants to say about itself, its products, and its services.

When it comes to a news or feature story in the editorial columns of the paper, though, or when someone is interviewed on television or radio, this is an entirely different matter. Why? Because "everyone knows" that this space or time is free, and because most of us believe what the media tell us. Right?

BE WARNED, HOWEVER: PUBLICITY IS NOT A PANACEA

It would be wonderful if the image created by publicity could cure all ills, but it can't—at least not for very long. The media certainly aren't stupid nor are consumers.

No matter how terrific your publicity is, it can't sell an inferior product or an unreliable service for very long. It can't erase an image created by unfriendly or dishonest employees. Publicity may give you a momentary advantage, but it won't last unless you change the facts to fit the publicity.

If you want your publicity to work for you, if you want publicity to improve your image with your various publics, then you'd better make sure that you are what you claim to be.

FIRST, DETERMINE THE IMAGE YOU WANT TO PROJECT

What image do you want to get across? There are an almost unlimited number of images that publicity can project for a company, product, or service. What sort of image do you want for your company? What about reliable, honest, technically competent, friendly, service-oriented, conservative, old-fashioned, up-to-date, trendy or "in," aggressive, high-quality, expensive, inexpensive, helpful, considerate, steady, or something entirely different? Before going any further, first make this decision.

BEGIN BY BEING WHAT YOU WANT TO APPEAR TO BE

In this area, perhaps more than any other, actions speak louder than words. You prove reliability by being reliable—and letting your customers know it. You prove friendliness by being friendly—and finding ways to get the word around. You prove your ability to lead a new technological advance by making technological breakthroughs and reporting them.

Once you decide on the image you want—the image that will increase sales—then make sure that image is reflected through your activities. For example, if you want your company and products to come across as on the cutting edge of technology, but your advertising, your headquarters building, and even your sales reps are stodgy and old-fashioned, the image of your product and company becomes confused.

IDENTIFY YOUR TARGET AUDIENCE

The goodwill of everyone even remotely associated with your company is indispensable. This means not only that the buying public should have a good feeling about your company and its products, but so should your employees, the community in which your company is located, your dealers, distributors, and suppliers, and your stockholders—even the government.

It doesn't take much knowledge about publicity to see that each "public" is probably influenced by a different type of action, story, or media. For example, should the company that manufactured my skin care product have updated its image? Of course. Even though I now have the negative image of the company as a bunch of upstarts making changes simply for the sake of change, I'm a customer who is already hooked. I'm not going to stop using the product just because of the package.

In the meantime, the more up-to-date product image can pick up a lot of new, younger customers. This is good business—if the younger audience hears about the product and is sold on the new image.

However, if the company has failed to get publicity for this new trendy image to inform and sell a younger audience, then it has wasted its efforts. Handled correctly, the publicity would be found in the magazines read by teenagers and young adults, on television shows watched by them, and on radio shows they listen to.

SELECT THE MEDIA BEST SUITED TO REACH YOUR AUDIENCE

Depending upon the audience you wish to reach, you may have to send out several different stories to several different media.

For example, where would John Diggs send publicity on his new Back to Basics promotional theme? To any editor or publication interested in saving the environment, of course. You also might send your publicity to a business editor, but you wouldn't normally send this sort of information to a financial editor—unless it affects profits—and then the stockholders (if you have them) would certainly want to know about it first.

HOW TO GET PUBLICITY FOR A NEW PACKAGE DESIGN

A new package design makes terrific photographs as well as copy. Have professional photographs taken of both the old and the new package. If yours is an old and reliable product there may have been several package design changes. Get a picture of all of them in their proper order. Underneath these photographs include the date the package design was developed. Set the latest design off a bit to highlight it.

Provide a brief history of the product's package design, and illustrate it with photographs. Explain why each design was selected.

A TRADEMARK IS DESIGNED EXPRESSLY TO CREATE AN IMAGE

An effective trademark reflects a company's total image. When you get publicity for your trademark, what you are really doing is telling the reader how you view yourself as well as how you wish to be perceived.

Trademark design is a fascinating study in itself. If you have a new trademark or if a new trademark is being designed for your company, take advantage of all the design elements of this type of story.

■ Save all sketches for a feature story, then feature the final design and explain why it was the one selected.

■ Show how the trademark or logo is used on all packages or stationery, and get photographs of the entire line.

■ Interview the designer, and get statements about why the artist portrayed the image of the company in this way.

■ Interview the company executives, and determine why this particular trademark was selected.

■ Pull out all the old logos, and show progress as your company grew and changed.

■ Use these designs as visuals for television interviews.

TELL THEM YOU'RE ON THE CUTTING EDGE OF THE NEW TECHNOLOGY

First you prove you are on the cutting edge of technology by coming out with and reporting on new products that demonstrate your technological breakthroughs. Send out new product announcement stories and photographs to every possible interested editor and publication. Also, arrange for television interviews on which you can, if feasible, demonstrate the new product.

Send out research and development stories. This tells customers that you are on the cutting edge of the industry. You have the image of advanced technology and of being a leader by consistently coming up with good new ideas. You can do this by developing research and development stories and any technologically oriented stories.

TELL THEM YOU HAVE THE BEST POSSIBLE PEOPLE WORKING FOR YOU

Announce all new and promoted personnel. The people you hire or promote say volumes about your company and the direction in which it is headed. For promotions and appointments, be sure to stress those qualifications that let the consumer know in which direction your company is heading.

If you hire someone for the position of vice president in charge of product control, what does this say about the quality of your product? Former jobs—the job just left—indicate the expertise and experience now offered to your company's customers.

TELL THEM YOU SUPPORT THE SALE OF YOUR PRODUCTS AT EVERY LEVEL

When you report a new advertising campaign, sales promotion program, and promotional materials, you're not merely relating facts, you are telling your distributors that your company helps them move the product off their shelves.

TELL THEM YOU'RE A GROWTH COMPANY

The reasons you are relocating, renovating, or constructing a new facility say a lot about your company. You are expanding to such a degree that you have outgrown your old plant or offices. You are becoming more streamlined. You are offering a new product and need new manufacturing space. You will be giving better services from your new facilities, expanding to accommodate an influx of new business, predicting the opening up of a new market, moving closer to your market and/or your suppliers: the list goes on and on.

TELL THEM YOU'RE SUCCESSFUL

Your buying public likes to know they are doing business with a company that is financially sound. Publicity that gets this message across might be news of your sales and earnings, a dividend, or a stock split, or perhaps a merger or acquisition.

Good financial publicity is one of the best methods available for improving your company's image with your stockholders. This is news that enhances your company's identification and prestige, draws positive customer attention, and in general improves your image within the financial community.

It tells your customers that yours is a well-run company and that you will be around if and when they need you again.

TELL THEM YOURS IS A QUALITY PRODUCT OR SERVICE

Unlike many consumers, purchasing agents for industrial products do not buy on impulse. For them quality includes performance, packaging, technical service, storage life, materials, in-plant handling characteristics, installation, and overall efficiency. Use every opportunity at your disposal to get these messages across.

Keep a constant lookout for customers who indicate that they like your product—for whatever reason. Watch your mail for testimonials, and have your salespeople report any and all compliments from customers.

Case histories that get these messages across are among the best image makers available. A good reason that most customers agree to release such a case history is that when you get publicity for your company, you get publicity for your customer as well.

TELL THEM YOU'RE RELIABLE

Your customers and the public in general have an image of your reliability because you are consistently reliable. Give your company an image of reliability, honesty, and integrity.

- You have a new replacement service? Report it.
- You have exceptional guarantees and warrantees? Send out news releases.
- You installed quality control procedures? Report them.

TELL THEM YOU'RE HIGHLY REGARDED IN YOUR PROFESSION OR INDUSTRY

Awards and citations, especially those given by your own industry, should be highly regarded since they indicate good judgment on the part of your peers.

TELL THEM YOU'RE A GOOD NEIGHBOR

Look around you. There is always some need to which your product can be put in a dramatic way, probably for nothing. If this is done the right way and reported accurately and adequately, you will receive more than a fair return on your costs. Do your civic duty, and then make sure the proper people and journals hear about it.

Does your company have the reputation for being cold and uncaring? Involve your personnel in civic duties, and report what they are doing.

TELL THEM YOU'RE FRIENDLY
You have an image of friendliness and helpfulness by consistently being friendly and helpful. A rude salesperson can demolish a company's image of friendliness. Consider giving special "friendship" awards to your employees.

CHAPTER PERSPECTIVE
In this chapter, we gave you methods for understanding the phenomenon of the company and product image and how to make it work for you.

INTRODUCTION AND MAIN POINTS

This chapter teaches you how to become your own creative imitator: how you can discover unexpected new markets for your product or service and serve these markets before someone else beats you to the publicity punch.

After studying the material in this chapter:

■ You will have a feel for using publicity to generate ideas for new and unexpected product uses.

■ You will learn how to find potential new markets among your past orders and incoming mail.

■ You will understand the occasional need to use new product features to attract a new market.

■ You will be prepared for the possible necessity of using price cuts to interest new market segments.

■ You will learn how to use new trends as a means of opening new market segments.

■ You will brush up on how to tap valuable employee ideas.

■ You will learn why product education may be necessary to open up new markets.

■ You will be acquainted with the need for making special offers in targeted industries.

■ You will learn how a seminar can generate all sorts of new market publicity.

■ You will learn how new geographic areas may provide you with your best new markets.

Many years ago I knew a young man who was always inventing something. Most of his inventions were practical. Some of his ideas were terrific and, I thought, definitely marketable. Years later I ran into his wife. I asked what he had done with his inventions.

"Oh," she laughed, "they're all up in the attic gathering dust."

That bothered me. It eventually led to the writing of a small business manual telling inventors and other small entrepreneurs how to use publicity to help market their new products. I got publicity in the media I assumed the "little guy" would read. Did any of these items attract the little guy? The inventor? Not many. At first the book barely sold.

Not about to give up, I sent copies of the book to the trade media in many different fields. It received good reviews, and orders began pouring in. So, where did they come from? The small inventor? No. From the top executives of some of the country's biggest corporations.

I had aimed for and missed my intended market. It was publicity that helped me find the perfect market niche for my small business manual.

How many markets for your product are out there that you haven't touched, perhaps haven't even considered?

IS THERE REALLY ONLY ONE MARKET FOR YOUR PRODUCT?

Most products are designed for a single purpose, for one specific market. If it doesn't sell in that market, some of us feel let down, even betrayed.

"Just think of all the time I spent trying to help you and now you say you don't want it!"

You're hurt. You're demoralized. So what do you do? Store it in the attic and forget about it? Don't you dare!

Find another market!

What if your product is successful in one market? Two markets? More markets?

Find yet another!

IF YOU DON'T SERVE THE NEW MARKETS, SOMEONE ELSE WILL

Always keep in mind that when it comes to any reasonably successful product, there is always a creative imitator hanging around in the wings. If there is a rapidly growing market niche for your product out there or if there are special-interest markets you have not identified or satisfied, one of these creative imitators will. This seems to be a law of the marketing jungle.

It makes sense, it seems to me, that you look at your product or service from the viewpoint of the customer in many potential markets. Consider new applications, a specific need that your product or service can satisfy or a beneficial end result that it can produce. In other words, become your own competitor.

There are never too many markets for your product. Never limit your sales. Don't let yourself become blind to possibilities. Don't let someone else get the upper hand on your potential new markets. Do it yourself!

BEGIN WITH A NEW PRODUCT USE

Ideas for new product uses can come from anyplace, many of them totally unexpected.

I remember, when I first began introducing new products on television and radio talk shows around the country, I was always surprised to be called to the telephone after a show in a city far away from home. The first thing that always went through my mind was, "Who in the world knows me here?"

In only one instance was it a friend from the past. All the other calls were from viewers or listeners who had suggestions for new product uses.

Each time I got an interesting suggestion, I checked it out—or had someone at the company check it out—to make sure it was a sound, promotable suggestion. When it turned out to be a good and practical idea, I reported it on the next television and radio interview shows, either talking about it or demonstrating it.

The call-ins I received were unexpected. Considering this, just think how many call-in ideas you might get if you made it a point to ask for suggestions, perhaps even offering a product or cash for each suggestion that proved to be practical and usable.

GET NEW PRODUCT USE IDEAS FROM FADS AND TRENDS

Each time I'm in the park and see people of all ages riding bicycles for pleasure and exercise, I am reminded that at one time bicycles were primarily used as a means of transportation. Some years ago when people began to have more leisure time, many began to think in terms of improving the quality of their leisure time, as well as their health.

Bicycle manufacturers spotted this trend, recognized it as a "new market," and promoted the heck out of their product for recreational purposes. Publicity not only alerted the general public to the bicycle's potential, but it also kept the trend alive and pumping.

These days when I see an elegantly dressed man come out of a Park Avenue apartment building, put on his helmet, get on his bicycle, and take off for his Wall Street job, I am startled. Maybe it's because of our growing concern over the environment, or perhaps it's because so many of us are interested in improving our health, but there doesn't seem much doubt about it—the bicycle as transportation seems to be today's new market.

When considering your own product, remember that it's just possible that a new trend, or even a new fad, may open up a new market for your product. If so, latch onto it and promote it with all the means and media at your disposal.

CHECK OUT PAST ORDERS
New products have an edge because they are still news and can command publicity as news, but don't give up hope simply because your product has—like the bicycle—been around awhile.

Mature products have another type of advantage. Over time they have piled up orders, and if you review these orders, you often discover that your product is being ordered for and used in ways completely foreign to its original intent.

ALERT YOUR ORDER TAKERS TO KEEP A LOOKOUT FOR THE UNEXPECTED
Check with your telephone operators and order takers. You will be surprised how many ideas current customers have for new product uses. Encourage your order takers and operators to take note of all these ideas and pass them along to you.

Be sure to get the names and addresses of those with product use ideas and send them a personal thank-you note. All of us like to be praised, and you may be the winner. After all, creative people seldom stop at one idea.

WATCH INCOMING MAIL FROM SATISFIED CUSTOMERS
There's a little of the "savior complex" in each of us. If we come up with a great idea, most of us like to share it. Like the viewer or listener who calls in after a talk show, many users, on their own, unexpectedly come up with new product use

ideas. Very often they write to the company to share the thought.

Don't let these letters slip through the cracks. Not only can they provide possible new uses, but with these people's written permission you might be able to use the customer's own words in a press release. Valuable? You bet it is.

EMPLOYEES ARE OFTEN A GOLD MINE OF IDEAS

Because they are around the product day in and day out, because they have access to companies with all sorts of possible product uses, your own company's salespeople and field representatives may well be a prime source of new market ideas.

Many companies make the product available to all their employees at little or no cost and, as a result, find that they benefit from employee suggestions. At any rate, make your employees aware that you are looking for practical new product uses: potential new markets that might have been previously ignored may suddenly come into focus. Incidentally, rewards for good suggestions are certainly in order.

CONSIDER PROVIDING YOUR PRODUCT TO SCHOOLS

Have you ever considered enlisting the services of schools to help you develop new markets? Have you ever really considered the publicity advantages of having your product available for use in schools? Just consider that in one public relations gesture, you have tapped a tremendous source of present and future buyers—both students and teachers: through the students you have gained access to the buying habits of parents, and as students grow up and enter the adult buying markets, you have the added advantage of a long-range potential for new markets.

Schools of all types from preschool to special training courses are always looking for ways and means of helping their students learn more about the products on the market. Give serious thought to offering your product to one or more schools as an important medium of publicity.

Component products, such as food ingredients, have long been offered to cooking classes. More and more high-tech companies provide educational institutions with products—computers and word processors—so they can become familiar with the product early in their buying lives.

SCHOOLS HAVE DEVELOPED NEW PRODUCT USES MORE THAN ONCE

Yours is a construction product—a basic building material. You might give product samples or a product kit to schools, teachers, and students, who might come up with new uses and, consequently, new markets. Remember, you're using their brains, so make sure they are compensated appropriately. Awards come to mind.

Your publicity comes in as you send out a news release announcing that you have presented these kits to schools and offer to send the kits to more schools. Certainly, you announce any contest and its winners in the media.

You take in-school photographs as students work on the projects. You build a complete promotion, with accompanying publicity, around the results of your promotion—the selection and award ceremonies.

All this not only promotes your company and its products, but it stimulates others to think of your product in new and exciting ways.

MAKE SPECIAL OFFERS IN TARGETED INDUSTRIES

You can often bring in new use ideas for your product by offering the product free. Advertising with its coupons does this all the time. So can publicity. If you want to see a good example, look at the new product section of any publication and watch television shows that get you to write in for things. Especially look at the trade publications. Here you find free literature being offered, free samples and free sample kits. Send a press release announcing your free offer to any media that might be even remotely interested.

A NEW PRODUCT FEATURE MIGHT OPEN UP A NEW MARKET

It may be that to really capture the attention of new market segment, you must come up with a new product feature. Certainly that's what a competitor would do to edge in on your product sales, so why don't you? Also, once you add the new feature you have an entirely new press release to send out about the new feature, as well as why it was added.

A PRICE CUT MIGHT OPEN UP A LOWER PRICED MARKET

It is well documented that a low price makes it unprofitable for any other company to compete with you by coming up with a similar product. Therefore, as soon as it is feasible, consider beating them to the punch—be the first to lower your price.

Be sure to keep potential new lower priced markets adequately informed through the publications they read, the television they watch, and the radio programs they listen to. Also notify fringe markets of the price reduction through the media that reach them.

AN OLD MARKET REOPENED IS LIKE A NEW MARKET FOR YOUR PRODUCT

From your sales department you can also obtain a list of all past purchasers. Compare this list with your current list of accounts, and see immediately those you have lost as well as those who are ordering less. Perhaps you can detect a pattern of sales lost, and why.

If your research indicates that something about the product or service needs to be changed or improved, or if you find that a new feature might solve an industry's problems, first add the new feature and then get your publicity about it in the appropriate media.

PRODUCT EDUCATION CAN OPEN NEW RETAIL MARKETS

This morning I read that a local store owner figured it would take her about four years to start making money on her crafts shop. The reason this made such an impact on me was that I had passed this very crafts shop on more than one occasion, and there was no one in the store except the owner. The owner also stated in the news story that she knew how to use every craft item in her store. Why, I wondered, doesn't she use those long, lonely hours in her store teaching others to use those craft items, as well?

A story in the local press could announce the classes. There would be no cost there. By teaching the classes herself there would be no charge there, either. At the same time she would be utilizing empty space and empty time and, very likely, helping to fill an empty till. After all, once someone knows how to use a new product, he or she will probably want to buy it. The new customer opens up a new market.

COMPLEX PRODUCTS REQUIRE CONSUMER EDUCATION TO OPEN NEW MARKETS

When I bought my word processor, I didn't buy it for its brand name, power, or speed. I bought the educational support and services offered by the company selling it.

If it weren't that I was given stacks of simplified educational materials, hands-on experience under the eyes of a patient and qualified instructor, and a toll-free telephone number I could call for emergency assistance, I would probably not own a word processor today. Now I don't know what I would do without it.

Was this a new product on the market? No, but it was a new product to me. Even before buying it I had to be convinced that I would be trained to use it properly and effectively. How did I learn about this product and these backup educational services?

I read about them in a consumer magazine!

A SEMINAR CAN GENERATE ALL SORTS OF NEW MARKET PUBLICITY

While browsing through a trade journal recently, I ran across a full-page advertisement announcing a seminar the company was about to hold. Well-known authorities in the industry would be speaking. The topics to be discussed were of importance to the industry: a natural for publicity. There would be lots of publicity. Right? Wrong.

I looked through the rest of the magazine. There was no story about the upcoming seminar. It wasn't even in the column listing the industry's seminars. What's more, there was nothing mentioned in the trade journal preceding this one, and there wasn't a single story in the following issue. What a wasted opportunity!

The company could have used this seminar to garner masses of free publicity—publicity to introduce the product to many potential buyers and new markets.

If you've ever looked through a trade publication you've probably seen seminars announced all over the country. Some publications even have special columns giving lists of them. There is no excuse for forgetting these publicity outlets when you plan a seminar. A seminar offers news stories, as well, whether for an industrial product or for a consumer product. Here are a few additional publicity ideas:

■ Hold a press conference. Invite the local media, the national wire services, and the trade press. Make them feel welcome. Set it up so that all the people invited as special speakers are there. Be sure to make press releases available, including biographies of each of your speakers.

■ Set up special television and radio interviews. Your speakers should carry enough weight to make them sought-after guests on the local television and radio talk show circuit. Talk with them in advance, and ask them if they have some special related subject they wish to discuss. Send bios and press clippings about the guest interviewee so the interviewer can ask informed and intelligent questions. Be sure to send an up-to-date press release about your seminar—the who, what, when, where, and why of it. Also, for goodness sake, remember to get a mention of your company and products. After all, this is why you are staging this seminar.

■ Arrange for television and radio interviews for executives from your own company.

■ Try for media coverage of the seminar. Try to set up at least one trend-setting session of interest to the media. Be sure to cover with your own professional camera people. Tape as many sessions as possible for later educational use, perhaps in schools or before workshops.

■ Invite an editor or reporter to attend the seminar. Many trade publications send reporters who will write long reports in their trade publications.

YOUR NEW MARKET MIGHT BE A NEW GEOGRAPHIC AREA

Geography and other demographic variables, such as climate, must often be considered to segment a market.

It is common practice today when a company introduces a new product for the company also to select only one sales territory at a time and concentrate on that. This automatically makes each new sales territory a new market. It also provides you with an entirely new geographic area in which to get publicity for your product.

Take the banana, for example.

The banana, under a variety of names, was an ancient fruit centuries before a man by the name of Jean Pouyat of Martinique brought this "new" product to the attention of agriculturists in tropical America a couple of centuries ago.

Now, how do you suppose he introduced this new product? Did he take out banana advertising in the local media, or perhaps in the agriculturists' trade publication? What about publicity? What about an important publicity tool—the demonstration?

Let's say that one day Jean Pouyat plopped a "hand" of bananas down in the middle of the street in Jamaica. What do you suppose happened? Well, of course, passersby probably became curious. They would undoubtedly have gathered around as this entrepreneur peeled a banana and ate it. If, then, the onlookers tried it and liked it, they probably took some bananas home for the family to taste.

Indeed, as it so happened, they liked the banana so much that agriculturists started to grow them. More new markets were subsequently opened. Is this the end of the story? Hardly. The other day I saw a batch of banana recipes in the morning paper, and just last night there was an impressive new television commerical touting the health benefits of the banana to senior citizens.

You see, even after centuries of "being around," the banana industry is still coming up with new promotional ideas to open up new markets. It is still increasing sales opportunities by coming up with new product uses and by tying in with new trends and growing market segments.

This just goes to show that regardless of how long your product has been around, there are always potential new markets out there.

Go get 'em!

CHAPTER PERSPECTIVE
Throughout this book we give you the means of getting media publicity. In this chapter, we gave you the means of getting the new ideas for product uses so that you can, in turn, use these new product ideas to generate additional media publicity.

How to Use Publicity to Presell Decision Makers

INTRODUCTION AND MAIN POINTS

In this chapter we concentrate on the person or persons who make the final money-spending decisions—how to identify them and how to presell them.

After studying the material in this chapter:

▬ You will learn how to identify the real decision makers.

▬ You will understand the importance of getting the selling facts to decision makers and how to do this.

▬ You will learn how to identify your superior sales message for a company's specific needs.

▬ You will learn how to presell an entire team of decision makers.

▬ You will learn how to select the best media to reach your decision makers, both professionally and geographically.

The owner of a large commercial cleaning company recently told me of a contract he had fully expected to get, but lost. He was devastated.

"It would have been a big contract," he said. "I had a good contact at this company. We actually became friends. I really thought I had the job; but when the time came to select a company, they chose my competitor. I was really upset. I spoke to my contact and he said, 'Bob, I'm so sorry, but I had no choice. You know I've only been here two years. I didn't want to make waves. The fact is, my bosses didn't know much about your company, so I went with the company we've always used. It was safer.'"

What if Bob had been on television and radio interview shows talking about his company and its work? What if some of Bob's satisfied customers had been interviewed for the trade publications or newspapers? What if customers had mentioned it after his company had cleaned the premises following a disaster? What if Bob, or someone else from his company, had been quoted in the trade press or on the business pages of the local newspapers, perhaps even in the national media?

What if . . .

IF YOU DON'T SELL THE DECISION MAKER, YOU DON'T SELL

Everyone makes buying decisions about one thing or another, from the mother shopping for groceries to the CEO hot after an acquisition. The process, however, is very much the same. They both want facts, and the closer they come to the moment of purchase, the more facts and details they want. It's up to you, the seller, to provide these facts and details.

GIVE THEM THE FACTS

It's possible that Bob's contact was simply a timid buyer. Certainly, a timid buyer has jinxed more than one sale.

It's possible that Bob's contact was, like many, not so much a designated buyer as a fact collector. It's also possible that important facts about Bob's company and services were inadvertently or perhaps even deliberately withheld from the real decision maker.

It's possible that his contact was making excuses for retaining Bob's competitor—for whatever reason.

On the other hand, all too often a sale is lost simply because the designated buyer doesn't get from the seller the facts necessary to make an intelligent decision or enough facts to pass along to the real decision maker. Whenever this is the case, it is a very expensive oversight.

To make any sale, you must not only have the superior product or service, but you must also know who will actually make the decision, and on what facts they will base that decision, and then see that the real decision makers have the necessary decision-making information.

PUBLICITY CAN HELP YOU IDENTIFY THE DECISION MAKER

When you sell a product for teenagers, it's natural to think that the teenager is the decision maker. Right? Not always. What about those expensive items—the bicycle, the motorbike, or even the car? Do you really think the teenager is the only decision maker? Hardly. Certainly not if someone else holds the purse strings; certainly not if someone is planning a gift. Teenagers undoubtedly have considerable input and influence, but they rarely make the final decision.

The same thing applies to companies. Users may have a major influence on the decision, but they may or may not be the decision makers.

PUBLICITY CAN HELP YOU DETERMINE WHO IS IN CHARGE—TODAY

There is another problem in today's business climate. The fact is, if there is one thing constant in business today, it is change. The decision maker who has been buying your products right along over the years may no longer be the decision maker. Indeed, you may not even know who the decision maker is. You don't dare alienate your current contact by going over his head—and even if you wanted to, you wouldn't know who to get to—or be able to reach her even if you tried. This is a triple bind.

PUBLICITY CAN HELP YOU SELL AN ENTIRE "TEAM"

When it comes to large ticket items, like vacations and homes, the entire family is involved in the decision. The same is often true in companies, especially in high-tech companies. In many instances decisions about products are centered around a project group. The buying may still be done through a centralized purchasing agent, but the actual "decision to buy" may rest with the project manager or some technical expert within a carefully selected team. This is the person—these are the people—you must reach. Also, this means that if your product can or will fit a wide variety of projects, you consequently have a wide variety of project heads to contact and sell.

PUBLICITY CAN GET YOUR COMPANY AND PRODUCT FACTS ON EVERY DESK

"No way," you might say. "If I went over the buyer's head—he'd crucify me!" Well, now, let's think about that.

You have a gut feeling that for your product, a very technical item, it is the user you must sell. First, though, you don't know who that person is, and even if you did, you're not at liberty to contact him. Aha! Yes, you are. With publicity! You don't even have to know his name. All you really need to know is what trade or professional publications he reads.

Say you happen to know that the real decision maker is the owner of the company, but even if your purchasing agent suggests it, you can't get past the owner's secretary. Yes you can—with publicity! All you have to know is what she reads, listens to, and watches on television.

PUBLICITY CAN SAFELY REACH OVER THE HEADS OF CURRENT CONTACTS

The first sales call at any company is generally made on a personal contact or on the purchasing agent.

Perhaps at the time you made your first call, your contact was the key decision maker. Perhaps now that contact's influence has been diminished by a merger, a new owner, or new and more influential elements in the company, or as in Bob's case, the contact has not been in the company long enough to make waves. Perhaps his influence doesn't cover the particular product you are selling. Your contact may not have the influence to do the actual buying, but he can certainly undermine your sales efforts.

Bob was right about one thing. After having made your first contact in a company, it is often difficult, even dangerous, to personally go over her head or around her to reach the individual who will actually make the decision to buy your product or service.

Publicity has no boundaries, no inhibitions, and no restrictions. Anyone who can read, listen, or watch can be reached and possibly influenced by publicity.

EVERY DOOR IS OPEN TO TARGETED PUBLICITY

Publicity can float over transoms and reach behind closed doors. Indeed, anyplace a newspaper can go, anywhere a magazine can go, anyplace television can invade, anywhere radio can be heard—this is where your publicity can be, even behind the closed doors of a president's office, limousine, or even home. Every time he or she picks up a newspaper or magazine, watches television, or listens to the radio, you have the opportunity to presell that decision maker.

When news about your company, product, or service is in the media that reach your decision maker, there is no such thing as a door that is closed to your sales message.

SELECTING YOUR BEST MEDIA AND YOUR BEST MESSAGE

Now that we have given you hope in reaching and pre-selling elusive decision makers, we find ourselves in the position of telling you that it will only work . . . if.

This is a big if. Publicity works if you get stories in the media that reach your decision maker. Publicity works only if you use those media to send the decision maker the message that presells him or her.

FIRST, CONSIDER THE CHOICE OF MEDIA

You know the product or service you are trying to sell. Do you also know precisely who will use it? This is an important starting point. Whether or not the user is the decision maker, you can bet that the user has important input in any decision, whether that decision maker is the head of the family or the head of a firm.

When a user—technical or otherwise—is about to make a serious purchase, you can bet he or she is reading the trade, professional, or special-interest publication that gives the most information, the most details. As I have said before, the closer that person is to the moment of purchase, the more facts and details he wants. Like cramming for a final exam, he'll generally "cram" for the big buy.

Now, these publications are in your field—your trade, profession, or special interest. Never forget, though, that the decision maker never stops reading her own trade, professional, or special-interest publications.

For example, let's say you are trying to sell enough new computers and software for an entire engineering department of a large corporation. Obviously you've had plenty of publicity on your product in computer publications, but have you gotten publicity on them in engineering publications? Have you made sure that professional engineering publications have carried case histories of the successful use of your computer and software in similar situations? Have you reported the special services you offer such customers?

This is just a sample of the sort of stories you might get in the user's publications of interest. Here is where you can double the preselling impact.

So, in addition to getting the facts about your product or service in your own media, determine just what media the user normally reads, and saturate those media with information—facts and details about your product and services.

LOCAL MEDIA REACH DECISION MAKERS IN THEIR HOMES

Also, keep in mind that everyone lives somewhere and almost everyone reads a local newspaper, watches local television, and listens to local radio. Especially when a decision is coming down to the line, when you have that terrible gut feeling you're running second, be sure to gear up to saturate the local media, that is, the local media of the decision maker as well as the local media of the business location. If a sale is very important to you, don't leave any stone unturned.

WHEN IT COMES TO THE SALES MESSAGE, TAKE YOUR BEST SHOT

Publicity that presells carries a specific sales message. Your sales message must be geared to the greatest want or need.

It is astonishing to me how much publicity gets in the media and does nothing but pat a company on its own back. You wouldn't waste advertising space this way, so why waste your publicity space? Media time and space are valuable. Make the most of them whether they are free or you have to pay for them.

You may have only one story to get your selling message across. Don't fritter it away. The problem is that in publicity, as in advertising, you can effectively use only one sales message at a time. It's possible that the sales message you use for others is the best for the targeted decision maker. Are you sure? Have you checked it out? If not, now is the time to do it. It's important.

TRY TO GET THE PRODUCT SPECIFICATIONS FROM THE COMPANY

Here is where your contact can help you. Study the target company's needs carefully. Try to determine where the user's most important need and your best sales point coincide. If this is the area in which your product or service is superior to your competitor's, you've just made a decision yourself. You've found your best selling message. If your competitor outstrips you in this area, find another area where you excel, and concentrate on that.

CONSIDER YOUR SALES MESSAGES

It really comes down to five basic sales messages: product superiority, service superiority, source superiority, people superiority, and, of course, price superiority.

Is your product really superior to that of your competitors? Now, be honest. This is vital. Are your product and the competitor's product about on a par? Perhaps your product is actually superior for many users, but perhaps not necessarily for this particular user. Well, then, maybe product superiority isn't your best sales message.

What about service? Is your customer service better? Would it be considered better by your targeted user?

What about the people who work for you? Are they better able to speak the language of the user? Would there be more rapport between the people in your company and in theirs? Do the people in your company have a higher level of respect in the field? Are they better known? Consider every possibility.

What sort of reputation does your company have? After all, source superiority is very important. Do you have a good reputation for integrity, for standing behind your product, for environmental concerns, for doing your civic duty? Weigh these and other factors when selecting your best and most competitive sales message.

Finally, we get down to price. This is often the best sales message of all. This doesn't mean that your product must be the least expensive. It may be that in lieu of a better reason, a user may well select the most expensive for prestige or perhaps even a greater sense of security.

Now, let's take each sales message and consider it in depth.

Product Superiority

Again I remind you that this doesn't necessarily mean that your product is superior in construction or even reliability. It may mean that it is superior simply because it is easier to use.

A superior product means superior in the eyes of the user—not necessarily superior in terms of objective values or according to laboratory standards. It also means superior to that of the competition.

So ask yourself, superior to what and in what what way?

In the announcement of a new or improved product, the tendency is simply to list the product's new features. To mark a product as superior, however, may mean that you must contrast your product with that of the competition.

SHOW HOW YOUR PRODUCT IS SUPERIOR FOR ITS INTENDED USE

What qualities does your decision maker consider superior?

In selecting the superior qualities of your product that you will push in your publicity, be sure that you select that quality or those qualities that the decision maker of a specific company considers superior for her own purposes, not merely what might be reported as superior by your contacts or your own technical personnel.

Let's say that one of the big selling points about your product is its flexibility. It can be used in a number of different ways. Obviously this is a good selling point. However, if your decision maker's company doesn't need flexibility in this product but is concerned with its ability to take abrasiveness, the message of flexibility won't sell. Don't waste your time, space, and effort on this point. Spend it on a product superiority the user cares about.

Also, be specific. When you describe your product's advantages and superior qualities, be as specific as possible. For instance, note the differences in these two sentences that might be used in your press release:

Our Company's (product) is durable and abrasion resistant.

Our Company's (product) affords five times the abrasion resistance of (competitive products) now on the market.

SOME QUESTIONS ABOUT PRODUCT SUPERIORITY TO ASK YOURSELF

If you can't get a person's or company's specifications for your type of product, if they are simply unavailable to you, consider your product in terms of what you believe would be the best qualities for that particular use. You might consider these points:

■*Space* is at a premium today in both homes and companies. Is your product designed so that it takes up as little space as possible? What about storage? Is it easy and convenient to store? Does it take an expert to remove it from storage, or can anyone do this? Photos demonstrating these features may be the best way to get this across.

▬ *Product versatility* is a big plus these days. In how many practical ways can your product be used? What about using it in different rooms for different purposes? Can more than one person use it? In addition to the obvious uses, what are some of the less obvious uses? Be imaginative; go through letters from users to get ideas. Ask your sales reps to keep their eyes and ears open for new ideas and new uses.

▬ *Saving time and money* is high on nearly everyone's list. Can you say that your product is more efficient and thus will save both time and money? Get examples and quotes from others who have found your product efficient for their purposes. Check with current users of your product. Consider reporting on case histories. Run a contest to prove the time-saving and money-saving qualities of your product. In your press releases, such phrases as the following can be very effective:

> The unit reduces waste because . . . .
>
> The (product) permits labor and management time for essential duties or early clock-out.
>
> (Product) eliminates mistakes associated with fatigue and "shortages" due to miscounts.

▬ *Safety* is a vital concern today whether in children's toys or in the most sophisticated machinery for multibillion dollar plants. Publicity can promote all the safety features built into your product.

▬ *Product design* in many products is the major sales message. Buyers want products that are attractive, more esthetic, products that come in many colors, styles, and sizes. Is your product more adaptable? Does it have special fittings? Does it have unusual applications? Does it have choices of power? Does it require less maintenance than that of your competitor? Feature this in a story.

▬ *Package design* has recently come under particular scrutiny not only for sales appeal but for safety as well. Is your product package safe? Is it attractive? Will it help move the product off the shelf? Report this.

▬ *Durability*: So many products today have built-in obsolescence that many decision makers are looking for products that are durable, that are unlikely to become obsolete, that have a longer life expectancy. To get these sales messages across you might aim for a book of records, consider an endurance test and promote it, locate and interview your oldest user, and think in terms of product anniversaries. Don't forget product warranties: are you ahead of the competition for guarantees and warranties—coverage and time duration? If so, say so, and provide any other proof that shows your company believes in and stands behind your product.

■*Extras*: Sometimes the "extras" can make the sale. For some a practical and protective cover might make the difference. For another product or decision maker, the announcement that the product comes with a case or rig might do the trick. Whatever it is, write it up, photograph it, and get the information to the user and/or the decision maker.

Service Superiority

This is a good area for preselling fast, and it is flexible. A new product can't be ordered up on a moment's notice, nor can an improved product. You can't come up with a better source than what you have at this moment, and you probably can't go out and hire someone for only a one-time sale, but you can come up with a service that specifically meets the needs of a particular decision maker and his company, a service that places your company and product out in front, away from the competition. When you find out what service is most needed, get some publicity for it—right now.

Whenever you can offer better service to a decision maker, this is bound to influence a decision maker's decision and, consequently, generate more business. From a decision makers' point of view, this is "value added." Make sure you take advantage of this.

As a product matures, there is less and less to talk about in terms of product superiority because the best is often imitated. Therefore, service often becomes an important factor in the sales-plus. If you don't have a superior service, you might be able to come up with one you'll be comfortable with, but be sure you can supply the service as promised and use this as the focus of your publicity.

Report all news from a service point of view. If service is the edge you are selling a decision maker, make sure that every possible bit of news that emanates from your company at least touches on the special service that you offer a decision maker's company. As you scan your company and its operations for superior people, product, or price, look at how it improves your service to your prospect. Then add this information to your press release.

PINPOINT THE SERVICE THAT WILL SELL YOUR DECISION MAKER

Here are a few questions to consider in judging both the services you currently offer your customers and those services you might add as an inducement to the decision maker.

■ *Technical assistance*: Do you back up your product with technical and other types of assistance? Does your technical staff solve technical problems for your customers? Are your field personnel trained and retrained regularly to keep them up-to-date? Have you increased your testing or research capabilities?

■ *Sales assistance*: Do you help your customers generate leads through direct or cooperative advertising? Are your merchandising deals, displays, or demonstrations superior to those of your competition?

■ *Training*: Following an installation, do you offer "start-up" training for operators? Consider, for example, the thought processes of a decision maker who is on the fence and then reads the following news about your company:

> Our Company has formed a training and education program specifically designed for "in-plant" presentation. The course offerings include:

■ *Delivery*: Is your delivery service faster, more frequent, or more convenient than the competition's? Are your distribution centers nearby? Are you located advantageously for shipping? Do you have a secure and convenient source of supplies? Do you own the necessary raw materials?

■ *Maintenance*: Do you provide superior maintenance policies and service contracts?

■ *Quality control*: Do you have special inventory practices—stock rotation, optimizing, and checking—that are important to industry in general and the customer in particular?

■ *Financial services*: Do you have the best credit terms? Do you offer the best financial sources and/or rates?

REPORT THAT YOU HAVE IMPROVED YOUR SERVICE

Obviously, no company has a perfect track record in all areas of service. Determine just where it is you need improvement, then do something positive about it. If you have been lax in providing adequate services to back up your sales staff, do something positive to remedy the situation, then report it. The fact that you have improved your services is a news story in itself. Be specific when reporting all improvements.

Publicity comes in by letting the decision makers know that you have done something about a problem—and just what that "something" is.

Superior Source

A company's reputation is often of prime importance in making a buying decision. Review the following points, and when you come across one or several that ring a bell, be sure to add it to your publicity.

■*Reputation*: Do you have a good standing in the industry, in the marketplace? Are your policies and practices known to be ethical, equitable, and consistent? Is your company viewed as a "good citizen" in the community? Is your company considered a good place to work? Is yours an old firm with experience, a feeling for history and tradition, or a new company with initiative and innovations? Does the competition imitate you? Have you scored any "firsts?"

■*Types of accounts*: Do you have prestige accounts in the same industry as the targeted user?

■*Employees*: Do you have skilled technicians or crafts personnel? Do you have good labor relations?

■*Financially sound*: Does your company have a good earnings and growth record? Is it financially sound?

■*Size*: Is your company large enough to have everything the user might want or need? Is it small enough to give the user individualized attention and service? Is your company growing? If you are renovating your place of business, constructing new facilities, or adding new equipment, don't just report this news—explain to decision makers how these changes will help them as customers.

People Superiority

Look around you at the people working in your company. They are top-notch, right? You know they are the best around, that through them your company can offer the best possible product and the best possible services to your customers.

If you can impart this knowledge to your decision maker—if you can make him or her believe it by proving it—then not only do you have a good news or feature story, you also have enormous influence with a decision maker. Your company has a powerful psychological advantage over your competition.

We keep going back to "all things being equal": what qualities do your employees have that your competition lacks? What is your strength? Are your people superior for the target company's needs?

■ *People skills*: Are your employees a source of good ideas for the target company? Are your people problem solvers?

■ *Experience in user's industry*: Do your people have proven knowledge and experience in the decision maker's industry? Do your people have technical knowledge about the products in use in the decision maker's industry?

Superior Pricing

The price of a product has many connotations to a decision maker. Whether yours is at the lowest end of the price scale or the highest, you can use this as a sales point—depending, of course, upon the company's and decision maker's needs.

■ *Prestige price*: Does price contribute to the symbol of your product? Are you selling a decision maker who requires a "quality image"? Is yours a luxury product? Are you selling to a social strata in which the standard of living is generally high? Does your decision maker consider luxuries a necessity? To your decision maker, does a high-quality product mean a costly product, or does he or she believe that a fine article is an expensive article? Does your decision maker associate high price with status and prestige? Does your price reflect to your decision maker the maximum value for the money? Is the high price of your product the only way the decision maker has to judge the quality of your product? Is your decision maker more concerned about quality, prestige, and value than money?

■ *Economy price*: When considering your product, does the decision maker consider its purchase a "sacrifice"? Is your decision maker concerned about spending money? Is the low price the result of volume sales?

■ *Price advantages*: Do you offer unexpected discounts? Do you offer a superior price advantage when, say, there is a future delivery? Are your terms of payment particularly attractive?

■ *Perks*: Are installation costs absorbed by your company? Is freight prepaid? Are your warranties better than average? Are your services available at no extra charge? Do you have superior trade-in allowances?

SELECT YOUR PUBLICITY MESSAGES CAREFULLY
Obviously you won't be able to get press releases in the media on each and every one of your superior qualities, but learn to study your decision makers continually and select those benefits that best fit your customers' needs.

Like publicity itself, this is an unending but fascinating occupation.

CHAPTER PERSPECTIVE
In this chapter we zeroed in on those decision-making individuals and project teams that have the final say in whether your product is selected over all other products on the market. In previous chapters we stressed the technical skills of getting publicity. Here we gave you definite targets upon which you might best ply those skills.

Bibliography

Behrens, John C.: *The Typewriter Guerillas (Closeups of 20 Top Investigative Reporters)*, Nelson-Hall, Chicago, Illinois, 1977.

Bernays, Edward L.: *Biography of an Idea: Memoirs of P.R. Counsel*, Simon & Schuster, New York, 1965.

Bernstein, Carl and Bob Woodward: *All the President's Men*, Simon & Schuster, New York, 1974.

Blyska, Jeff and Marie: *PR, How the Public Relations Industry Writes the News*, McGraw-Hill, Inc., New York, 1975.

Chancellor, John and Walter R. Mears: *The News Business*, Harper & Row, Inc., New York, 1982.

Dilenschneider, Robert L.: *Power and Influence (Mastering the Art of Persuasion)*, Prentice Hall, Inc., New York, 1990.

Dilenschneider, Robert L. and Dan J. Forrestal: *Public Relations Handbook*, 3rd Edition, The Dartnell Corporation, Chicago, Illinois, 1987.

Hill, John W.: *Corporate Public Relations, Arm of Modern Management*, Harper & Row, Inc., New York, 1958.

Hill, John W.: *The Making of a Public Relations Man*, David McKay Co., Inc., New York, 1963.

Iacocca, Lee with William Novak: *Iacocca, an Autobiography*, Bantam Books, New York, 1984.

Jeffries, James R. and Jefferson D. Bates: *The Executive's Guide to Meetings, Conferences and Audiovisual Presentations*, McGraw-Hill, Inc., New York, 1983.

Lesley, Philip, editor: *Lesley's Public Relations Handbook*, Prentice Hall, Inc., New York, 1983.

Nessen, Ron: *It Sure Looks Different from the Inside*, Playboy Press, New York, 1978.

Pinsdorf, Marion K.: *Communicating When Your Company Is Under Siege*, D.C. Heath & Co., Lexington, Massachusetts, 1987.

Parkinson, C. Northcote and Nigel Rowe: *Communicate, Parkinson's Formula for Business Survival*, Prentice Hall, Inc., New York, 1978.

Simons, Howard and Joseph A. Califano, Jr., Editors: *The Media and Business*, Vintage Books, New York, 1979.

Wallace, Mike and Gary Paul Gates: *Close Encounters, Mike Wallace's Own Story*, William Morrow & Co., Inc., New York, 1984.

Warner, Rawleigh, Jr., and Leonard S. Silk, Editors: *Ideals in Collisions (The Relationship between Business and the News Media)*, Columbia University Press, New York, 1978.

Wood, Robert J. with Max Gunther: *Confessions of a PR Man*, New American Library, New York, 1988.

Index

More selected BARRON'S titles:

ACCOUNTING HANDBOOK, Joel G. Siegel and Jae K. Shim
Provides accounting rules, guidelines, formulas and techniques etc. to help
students and business professionals work out accounting problems. Hardcover:
$29.95, Canada $38.95/ISBN 6176-4, 832·pages

REAL ESTATE HANDBOOK, 3rd EDITION
Jack P. Freidman and Jack C. Harris
A dictionary/reference for everyone in real estate. Defines over 1500 legal,
financial, and architectural terms.
Hardcover, $29.95, Canada $39.95/ISBN 6330-9, 810 pages

**HOW TO PREPARE FOR THE REAL ESTATE LICENSING
EXAMINATIONS-SALESPERSON AND BROKER, 4th EDITION**
Bruce Lindeman and Jack P. Freidman
Reviews current exam topics and features updated model exams and supplemental
exams, all with explained answers.
Paperback, $11.95, Canada $15.95/ISBN 4355-3, 340 pages

**BARRON'S FINANCE AND INVESTMENT HANDBOOK,
3rd EDITION,** John Downes and Jordan Goodman
This hard-working handbook of essential information defines more than 3000 key
terms, and explores 30 basic investment opportunities. The investment
information is thoroughly up-to-date. Hardcover $29.95, Canada $38.95/ISBN
6188-8, approx. 1152 pages

FINANCIAL TABLES FOR MONEY MANAGEMENT
Stephen S. Solomon, Dr. Clifford Marshall, Martin Pepper, Jack P. Freidman and
Jack C. Harris
Pocket-sized handbooks of interest and investment rate tables used easily by
average investors and mortgage holders. Paperback
Real Estate Loans, 2nd Ed., $6.95, Canada $8.95/ISBN 1618-1, 336 pages
Mortgage Payments, 2nd Ed., $5.95, Canada $7.95/ISBN 1386-7, 304 pages
Bonds, 2nd, Ed., $5.95, Canada $7.50/ISBN 4995-0, 256 pages
Canadian Mortgage Payments, 2nd Ed., Canada $8.95/ISBN 1617-3, 336 pages
Adjustable Rate Mortgages, 2nd Ed., $6.95, Canada $8.50/ISBN 1529-0, 288 pages

All prices are in U.S. and Canadian dollars and subject to change without notice. At your
local bookseller, or order direct adding 10% postage (minimum charge $3.75, Canada
$4.00), N.Y. residents add sales tax.   ISBN PREFIX 0-8120

Barron's Educational Series, Inc.
250 Wireless Boulevard, Hauppauge, NY 11788
In Canada: Georgetown Book Warehouse
34 Armstrong Ave., Georgetown, Ontario L7G 4R9   R 10/94

More selected BARRON'S titles: